Buy Unlimited Properties and Retire in 10 Years

Mark Reister

About the author

Mark Reister first became interested in real estate when he sold his second home in Perth, Western Australia. After returning home to Victoria, he pursued a career as an estate agent and in 1993 began work with Woodards Real Estate.

He met his wife Trudie while holidaying overseas, and the two now live with their son and daughter in Shepparton, a small regional city two hours' drive north of Melbourne.

After the move to country Victoria, a brief break from selling real estate saw Mark deepen his interest in property investment. Inspired by the people who would come back to him year after year to buy property after property, he strove to understand how it was possible to buy *unlimited* investment properties. In his first book, *How to Buy Unlimited Investment Properties* (2013), he shared the story of how he eventually built his own investment portfolio, along with the knowledge you can use to do the same.

Mark is now the part owner of a real estate office, Professionals McNamara, Thompson, Reister.

He remains devoted to real estate and to helping others learn how to reach their property investment goals. This, his second book, focuses on how you can build and generate income from your property portfolio to achieve financial independence and retire in just 10 years.

Contents

List of figures

9

List of tables

Acknowledgements

To my editor, Ben Hourigan, my family, friends, and those people who read *How to Buy Unlimited Investment Properties* and gave me their comments and so much positive feedback, thank you.

After finishing my first book, at first I could not have imagined I would write a second. Without your overwhelming support and encouragement, together with the occasional push in the right direction, I would never have contemplated, let alone written, this book.

I hope that you enjoy it and find it worth the wait.

1. You can retire in 10 years

Making plans, dreaming of the future, ambition, and drive are just some of the qualities that make humans different from other animals. We all have them to varying degrees. At some time in the past, we have all dreamt of winning the lottery or of what we would do if we suddenly found an extra million dollars in our bank account.

If you are reading this book, and if you've read others like it, you have almost certainly dreamt of using real estate as a vehicle to make your fortune. If you have not yet bought an investment property, there is no better time to start than now, as I also explained in my first book, *How to Buy Unlimited Investment Properties*.

If you *have* already bought one or more investment properties, well done! But now what? Sometimes we get so focused on the journey that we lose sight of our ultimate goal. At other times, we can be so absorbed in what we want to achieve that we get lost on the way or, worse, become paralysed and don't know where to start.

In *How to Buy Unlimited Investment Properties*, I

explained how I acquired my investment portfolio, step by step. Along with many other important issues, that book covers topics such as:

- how to search for suitable properties
- how to carry out due diligence
- how to prepare a comprehensive financial analysis
- how to negotiate with valuers and estate agents
- why you should use the services of a quantity surveyor
- the importance of insurance
- how to secure bank finance
- the benefit of forming a syndicate to buy properties at genuinely discounted prices

In *this* book, which follows on from my first but can just as well be read on its own, I cover many further topics that I believe are crucial for maintaining a healthy investment property portfolio but receive little fanfare or discussion.

Before acquiring my investment portfolio, I attended numerous property investment seminars and read scores of books on the topic. These usually concentrated on buying properties, and to some lesser extent on *why* you should buy properties. But if you have bought investment properties, what should you do now? Should you hold onto them forever? Should you self-manage your properties, or use a property manager from a real-estate agency? Should you sell them? Those are just some of a host of frequently asked questions.

Having worked as a real-estate agent for the past two decades, and now being the owner of a real-estate agency, I have been asked these questions by property investors. If you know the answers, it will make managing your portfolio a whole lot easier and more enjoyable. In fact, knowing will make having an investment portfolio a pleasure rather than a chore.

It's easy to pick out the property investors who have a clear idea of what they want to achieve from their portfolio: they are enjoying themselves and not stressing. They don't constantly second-guess themselves. When they decide to do something, like buying another property or selling a property, they do it confidently without procrastinating, and they get the result they want.

You can also quite easily pick out those property investors who do not have a clear picture of what they want to achieve. These are the people who frequently ask questions like, "Should I sell? Should I buy more properties? What is happening in the real-estate market? Are prices going up or down?" What do you think is going to happen with interest rates?

Many of these investors probably already know the answers to most of their questions, but they continually second-guess themselves and look for others to take the lead, which leads to self-doubt, insecurity, and ultimately stress.

Often these investors end up selling their investment property, but if you ask them why, they don't have any great insights or answers. In such a sale, this type of investor often makes little or no profit once all costs incurred in buying and selling the property have been taken into account. These people will usually tell you that investing in real estate is bothersome, that you will have problems with tenants, and that making money from real estate is difficult. Basically, they will tell you every horror story there is to hear or read about real estate.

For obvious reasons, these are not the people you want to take advice from. If only they had a little clarity about what they wanted to achieve, property investing would have been a lot easier and more enjoyable. Most millionaires have amassed their fortunes with the help of real estate, and much of their wealth is in property, so the process cannot be all that bad.

Having a clear picture of what to do after you have bought investment properties will allow you to sit back, relax, and let the properties do the rest of the work. Even if you are not physically working on your investment properties, you are still working if you are constantly thinking about them or, worse, worrying about them. You have to be able to stop thinking about your properties if your investment portfolio is truly going to provide you with a passive income on which you can retire and enjoy life.

When we go on a holiday, a lot of people (including myself) still think about work. We worry about the jobs we have left unfinished. We think that our workplaces cannot function without us, because we are indispensable. But we should be relaxing. Thankfully, after a few days of these holiday worries, we usually switch off mentally and forget about work temporarily. Then we really start to relax and enjoy the break. We need to be able to reach this kind of situation with our investment portfolios. If you're still worrying about it, you're still working. And that kind of stress can lead to significant health problems, so you want to avoid it.

Your investment properties will look after themselves. They will grow in value regardless of how much time you spend looking at them or thinking about them. That is one of the major attractions of real estate as an investment. Historically, it always goes up. In my first book, *How to Buy Unlimited Investment Properties*, I provided several pages of tables giving 50 years of statistical evidence to illustrate this very point.

Over a 50-year period in Melbourne and Sydney (1960–2010), representing 100 distinct years of sales results, the median house price dropped only 15 times (seven times in Melbourne and eight times in Sydney). House prices increased in 85% of the years considered. If you own investment properties, you really can relax—they will increase in value even if you do nothing.

But that doesn't mean you can close your eyes. There are important issues you should not ignore, and in the following pages, I'll let you know what they are and how to deal with them, so you can do what you need to and get back to relaxing.

In this book, I cover many topics that are crucial for you to understand so you can ensure the health of your investment portfolio. But it's likely that there will be some questions I won't cover—probably relating to your specific personal circumstances. If you encounter issues like these, please seek professional advice: almost any issue or problem you encounter will be something that others have previously seen and dealt with.

Asking for help should not be a source of embarrassment. Many, many people have helped me throughout my life, in my career and with my investment properties, and I'm very grateful to them.

Better yet, others whose advice you follow will usually feel a great sense of pride, especially when you succeed—as the saying goes, "imitation is the highest form of flattery." Just make sure that your advice comes from someone who has achieved what you want to achieve, not from one of this world's many doomsayers.

Hold or sell?

Let's say you've bought an investment property, or better yet, properties. What should you do now? Do you sell and make some money, or should you hold your investments and live off the rental income? This is a fundamental question, at the heart of your investment strategy.

Plenty of people, including so-called experts, will happily give you advice about whether you should hold or sell. There is no one correct answer for all of us. Quite simply, the choice comes down to you. It depends on how you feel and what you want to achieve. That's not to say that you should not seek advice and discuss your options with other people, but no one other than you (and perhaps your family) will have to live with the choices you make. So—you will need to do what you feel is best, given your circumstances.

If you choose to sell your investment property, you will obviously want to make a profit. This means that what you get from the sale will have to exceed the purchase price *and* the costs you incurred when you bought the property, while you owned it, and when you sold it.

To work out your profit or loss, you need to deduct all this from your sale price:

- the price you paid for the property
- all your acquisition costs (including stamp duty, conveyancing fees, and bank fees)
- all selling costs (including estate agents' fees, marketing fees, and conveyancing fees)
- all capital improvement costs (such as kitchen renovations, new tiling, landscaping, and painting).

Adding these to the price you paid shows you what the investment has really cost you.

You will note that I have not asked you to deduct ongoing costs like council rates, insurances, and interest on borrowings. These are treated differently from capital expenditure costs by the tax office, and are not taken into consideration when you are calculating your capital gain. A property owner can be effectively compensated for these costs through tax claims and tax deductions.

Similarly, many capital expenditure costs can be claimed in your personal income tax, and will therefore not be included in your capital gain calculations. However, when I am assessing the profit I have made after selling an investment property I still include these costs for my own reference. I have carried out these improvements with the belief and hope that they will increase the appeal and hence the value of my property, and I want to make sure that I am fully reimbursed for their cost when I sell.

As I mentioned, all acquisition costs, selling costs, and capital expenditure costs need to be taken into consideration for capital gain calculations. When you sell an investment property, you must pay tax on the capital gain (profit) that you have made. All capital improvement costs may be deducted from your sale price, reducing your capital gain and thereby your tax bill. However, be careful if you have previously claimed a capital gain cost in your personal income tax: you cannot claim it again in your capital gain calculation.[1]

---

[1]Many of the tax-related observations in this book are based on the situation current in Australia as of 2015. If you or your investment are in a different jurisdiction, you should check the tax rules that apply there. You should always, in any case, seek expert advice on matters related to taxation, from your accountant, professional financial adviser, or another relevant professional.

Below, in Table 1, I give you an example of how to calculate your capital gain after you sell an investment property.

Remember that capital expenditure items cannot be claimed in your personal income tax and again in your capital gain calculations. This example does not take into consideration items that you have claimed depreciation on (a topic covered in Chapter 2 of *How to Buy Unlimited Investment Properties*).

For many investors, selling an investment property is a very profitable and attractive option. The profit from selling can be used to live on, for buying other investments, or for anything else you have in mind. It's your money.

Many investors make a living from regularly buying and selling investment properties. These investors know the importance of finding a property at the right price: below its real market value. The property may have failed to attract the right price because it was poorly presented, or it may have been a mortgagor sale or a deceased estate sale that didn't receive the buyer interest it should have. Be aware that just because a property is being sold on behalf of the mortgagor or as part of a deceased estate, it doesn't automatically mean that it is being undersold. The real key is to know what properties are worth in the area—this means carrying out due diligence and

Costs	
Purchase price	$600,000
Stamp duty*	$31,070**
Conveyancing fee*	$1,500
Bank fee*	$1,000
Valuation fee*	$550
New kitchen	$10,000
New bathroom	$8,000
New carpets	$8,000
Painting	$7,000
Estate agent's fee[†]	$13,200
Marketing costs[†]	$6,000
Conveyancing fee[†]	$2,000
Total costs	$688,320
Sale price	$800,000
Less total costs	($688,320)
Capital gain (profit)	$111,680

*paid when buying
**Victorian stamp duty calculation for a property that is not your principal residence, based on a market value of $600,000
[†]paid when selling

Table 1: 1 Investment Street, Melbourne

having a thorough knowledge of property prices.

The kind of investor who regularly buys and sells investment properties typically scours the real-estate market looking for a bargain. These properties are usually poorly presented. Once they've bought the place, such an investor will then carry out cosmetic improvements like painting, gardening, carpeting, and tiling. Six to twelve months later, they resell the property and make their profit.

A cautionary note: this kind of buying and selling, often called *flipping*, is difficult to do in a stagnant or declining market. When property prices are naturally increasing, you can rely on your improvements *and* market growth to make a profit. If you buy at the right price, improve the property carefully without overspending, and prices are naturally increasing in the area then you should be confident of achieving a sale price that covers the purchase price plus all the added costs we've discussed above. That leaves you with a tidy profit for your troubles.

But when the real-estate market is in decline and prices are dropping, it becomes very difficult to increase your sale price enough to cover all your costs and make a substantial profit. For this reason, buy-and-sell investors vanish when the going gets tough, and appear again when the market as a whole begins to rise.

While flipping properties as a strategy has obvious attractions, and you can make a very good income from doing it, the big problem is that you can only sell a property once. When you have finished improving the property, sold it, and taken your profit, you need to start looking for the next property to repeat the process on. And the property you have just sold could be a goldmine—it might go up in value faster than other properties you might buy in years to come. In just a few years, the property you sold could turn out to have been someone else's bargain.

If you decide that you would like to make money from buying and selling real estate, you can take a look at Chapter 3 of this book for a discussion of what sort of property you should look for. Later, in Chapter 4, I tell you how to maximise your sale price.

If you would prefer to hold your investment properties, there are various strategies available and options that you need be consider. For example: how can you get money out of your investment without selling it? What's the best way to move on and buy *another* investment property?

If these questions occur to you, there are two options you should consider. One is refinancing. The other is paying off your investment property and living off the rental income.

Option 1: Refinancing

Many readers will already be familiar with refinancing. This is when you get a new, usually larger, mortgage to replace an existing loan you have against a property. The reason you would do this is to receive money in your bank account.

The downside of this strategy is that your debt has grown because you now have a larger loan, and your repayments will have gone up as well. But if the rental you receive from your investment property is enough to cover repayments on the new loan, refinancing is an effective way to get a lump sum of money from your property without selling it.

You can use the money you get from refinancing any way you like. You could live off the money, or buy other investments—the choice is yours—but remember, your mortgage is still a debt.

The advantage of refinancing as a strategy for extracting money is that you get to keep your property, which will continue to grow in value the longer you have it.

You can typically refinance your loan at any time, provided that your property has increased in value enough that you can still maintain the minimum required equity.

As an example, imagine you bought a property

for $500,000 with an 80% loan for $400,000. Now the property is worth $600,000. You could refinance this property by taking out a new 80% loan for $480,000. With that new loan, you repay the initial loan of $400,000 and still have an extra $80,000 in your bank account.

Using this strategy you could create a passive income stream in the next 10 years and RETIRE. Here is how it works:

Year 1

Buy an investment property for $500,000

Year 2

Buy an investment property for $500,000

Year 3

Buy an investment property for $500,000

Years 4–10

Repeat as above.

With 10 properties in your portfolio, in the eleventh year you would refinance the investment property you bought in Year 1. This property should have doubled in value, and as a result, it should be worth $1,000,000. Using the money you receive from refinancing, pay back the initial loan of $500,000 and live off the remaining $500,000. Repeat this step each year, always refinancing the property that is having its tenth anniversary. If you do this, you will never need to work again.

This is what the process looks like:

Year 11
Refinance property bought in Year 1. Get new $1 million loan and repay $500,000 loan. Live off remaining $500,000.

Year 12
Refinance property bought in Year 2. Get new $1 million loan and repay $500,000 loan. Live off remaining $500,000.

Year 13
Refinance property bought in Year 3. Get new $1 million loan and repay $500,000 loan. Live off remaining $500,000.

Years 14–20
Repeat as above.

This strategy does not have an expiration date. You can continue it indefinitely if you keep refinancing. The only thing that will change is that the dollar values involved will increase. For example:

Year 21

Refinance property bought in Year 1 and later refinanced in Year 11. Get new $2 million loan and repay $1 million loan. Live off remaining $1 million.

Year 22

Refinance property purchased in Year 2 and later refinanced in Year 12. Get new $2 million loan and repay $1 million loan. Live off remaining $1 million.

Year 23

Refinance property purchased in Year 3 and later refinanced in Year 13. Get new $2 million loan and repay $1 million loan. Live off remaining $1 million.

And so on...

Using this strategy, after the first 10 years you can live on an annual salary of $500,000, and after 20 years you can give yourself a pay rise and live on $1 million per year. If you keep repeating this process, the money involved becomes enormous. That is where many readers will see a problem.

The sceptics will say…

It's too easy. You need to buy more properties.

I say…

If you would like to buy more than 10 properties, go ahead. I've chosen 10 properties because it means you only need to buy one property each year. If you think of it this way, it is a relatively easy task.

The sceptics will say…

But the properties cannot keep doubling in value every 10 years.

I say…

Look at the property prices in Melbourne and Sydney over the past 50 years (see the appendix to *How to Buy Unlimited Investment Properties*). Similar results can be found in other capital cities around Australia.

Prices have gone up in the past, and they will continue to go up in the future. Even if they do not double every 10 years, and they increase by only 70% every 10 years, it still means that the investment property you paid $500,000 for in Year 1 is worth $850,000 in Year 10, giving you $350,000 to live on each year. After 20 years, the properties you are dealing in will be worth $1,445,000, allowing you to live on $595,000 per annum for the next 10 years. You can manipulate the increases to any percentage that you like. You can be as conservative or optimistic as you like. Regardless, this strategy can still be applied.

The sceptics will say...

The passive income of $500,000 after 10 years shown in the example above is too generous.

I say...

You can change the outcomes and projected passive income to what you believe is achievable and acceptable in your mind. Once you start on your path to creating your investment portfolio, you can keep adjusting your projections. Your passive income will change as you acquire more properties. When you believe you have enough properties to give you a passive income you are happy with, you can stop buying more.

The sceptics will say...

Buying one property a year for the next 10 consecutive years is too hard. It's unrealistic.

I say…

On the contrary, I believe buying one property a year is quite achievable. If you feel it is too hard, you can buy one property every two years. Instead of owning 10 properties after 10 years, you will have five. Based on the scenario I have described above, on the tenth anniversary of buying your first property you would still have $500,000 to live on but you would need to make it last two years, until you refinance your next property on its tenth anniversary.

The sceptics will say…

If this is so simple, why aren't more people doing it?

I say…

Most property investors do not have a clear plan or path that they are following. The refinancing option I have outlined requires a conscious, deliberate, methodical approach with a clear plan, timeline, and desired outcome.

I suspect most property investors do not follow this path simply because they are not aware that it is an option available to them. The statistics clearly show that most property investors own only one rental property. This is despite the fact that real estate underpins Australia's wealth. The total value of Australian real estate was recently estimated at $5.1 trillion by RP Data/Core Logic.

You can make a lot of money from owning a single investment property, but you can make *more* money by owning two, and if you own three you will be able to afford many of life's luxuries. If you own as few as five well-performing residential investment properties, you can set yourself up for the rest of your life with a regular, passive income and be on your way to retirement.

The sceptics will say...

The example above assumes a purchase price and loan of $500,000.

I say...

You can change the numbers to anything you like. If you change the purchase price to $400,000, after 10 years the property should be worth $800,000, and as a result you will have $400,000 to live on each year for the next 10 years.

If you want to make the purchase price $400,000 and you want a loan of $360,000 (assuming that you pay a 10% deposit when you purchase the property), after 10 years the property is still worth $800,000, you re-pay the loan of $360,000 using your new loan of $720,000 (assuming you keep 10% equity in the property), and live off $360,000 a year for the next 10 years.

~

This strategy may appear too simple for some readers. They will feel it should be more complicated or harder. But many millionaires around the world rely on this incredibly straightforward plan to make their living. They control assets, manipulate money, and let others service their debt.

In the example above, after 10 years you could control assets worth $5 million. In fact, the properties will most likely be worth considerably more than this, because you have already owned one property for 10 years, another for nine, another property for eight, and so on. If we assume a compounding annual growth rate of 7%, after 10 years your investment portfolio should actually be worth around $7,391,790.

What do you in fact own after you have bought these properties? Nothing, if you have used 100% borrowings. You are using the bank's money. As the owner, you are moving money around to create a passive income stream for yourself. You are manipulating the financial system.

There is nothing wrong, illegal or immoral in this. You found the properties in your portfolio through your own efforts. If your bank says they would like to see the loans paid down, you can always change banks. Lending money is a very competitive business, and there are many lenders who are looking for your custom, particularly when you control such a large investment portfolio.

Your portfolio is a business

I consider my investment portfolio a business where I am the CEO. My tenants are like employees. They work, make money, and pay rent to me, which I use to service the debt.

This may seem heartless or condescending towards my tenants, but I certainly mean no disrespect to them. I am grateful that they are renting one of my properties.

I look at my portfolio as a business because, just in like a business, there is income and expenses. I control the business and make sure that it is running smoothly. If repairs need to be done, I make sure they are done by a professional in a timely manner. If the business requires improvements or scheduled maintenance, I make sure that they are carried out. If a tenant has a grievance, I listen to their request.

My business needs enough tenants to ensure that the properties are filled and there are no vacancies.

This provides the income (rent), which needs to cover all outgoings (expenses). At the end of the year, a profit and loss statement is produced for my portfolio.

Like any business, my investment portfolio has to stay solvent. The income must pay for all of the expenses. I don't need to work directly in the business because I employ property managers who handle the day-to-day affairs of the properties, but any major decisions are referred to me as the CEO. Thanks to my tenants servicing the debt, the property managers who oversee the business, and my own prudent management, my business is solvent, self-sustaining, and profitable.

Challenges with refinancing

The difficult thing about this system of refinancing is that you need to keep a relationship with your bank and see them each year. Most likely, after a while you will get sick of applying for new loans.

The process of getting a new loan is cumbersome. Each time, you need to provide the bank with your full financial information, which includes documentation of your personal income (group certificate, tax returns, etc.) and all relevant information about your investment portfolio, which includes current valuations, rental agreements, income statements, and so on. This is certainly worth it when it achieves your desired outcome, but it can be laborious nonetheless.

The other problem with this system is that each time you refinance your investment property, it will have a significant impact on how your investment is geared. Until now, the interest you have paid on your loan has been tax-deductible, and this deduction has decreased the amount of tax that you have paid. If you refinance your investment property and then devote any part of the new loan to personal use, such as living expenses, the interest paid on this part of the borrowings can no longer be claimed as a tax deduction. As an example, if you buy an investment property for $500,000 and then after 10 years you refinance the property and secure a new $1 million loan, from which you take $500,000 to live on, you can only claim the interest paid on $500,000 in your tax return.

Tax laws relating to interest deductions also affect homeowners who want to turn their home (their principal place of residence) into an investment property. As an estate agent, I have very often met homeowners who wanted to move into a newly bought house while keeping their home as an investment property. To do this, the homeowner would refinance their existing loan and use the money from the new, larger loan to buy or build a new home. Unfortunately, the interest you pay on that new loan cannot be claimed as a deduction in your tax return, because the money from the new loan has been used for the personal reason of buying the new home. If you cannot claim the interest paid on the loan, your investment property is severely negatively geared and not a good investment.

To further illustrate this point on taxation, I have taken the example below directly from the Australian Taxation Office website.

Example: Interest incurred on a mortgage for a new home

Zac and Lucy take out a $400,000 loan secured against their existing property to purchase a new home on the other side of town.

Rather than sell their previous home they decide to rent it out.

They have a mortgage of $25,000 remaining on their existing home which is added to the $400,000 loan under a loan facility with sub-accounts – that is, the two loans are managed separately but are secured by the one property.

Zac and Lucy can claim an interest deduction against the $25,000 loan for their previous home,

---

as it is now rented out.

They cannot claim an interest deduction against the $400,000 loan used to purchase their new home as it is not being used to produce income even though the loan is secured against their rental property.[2]

This same ATO website has a section titled "Rental properties – avoiding common mistakes," which notes:

> There have been a number of common mistakes identified in the tax returns of rental property owners. ... If you use a loan facility for both investing and private purposes – for example, to purchase or renovate a rental property and to buy a motor boat – you cannot claim the interest expense on the private portion of the loan (the motor boat).
>
> A common mistake is to claim a deduction for interest on the private portion of the loan. [3]

[2] "Rental properties – claiming interest expenses", last modified 13 August 2014, www.ato.gov.au/General/Property/In-detail/Rental-properties/Rental-properties---claiming-interest-expenses/.

[3] ATO, "Rental properties – avoiding common mistakes",

Although there are issues like this that you need to consider when using refinancing, they do not diminish its merits as a strategy that can provide a passive income and a path to retirement.

The overwhelming benefit of this system, when compared with the option of simply selling, is that you keep the property, which will keep appreciating indefinitely and thereby provide you with an income source for the rest of your life.

Option 2: Pay off your investment property

This strategy is best described as a hybrid of the first two choices – "sell" and "hold." As I mentioned earlier, the worst thing about selling an investment property is that you can only make a profit from it once. You sell and have a big payday, but in a few years, if real-estate prices have rocketed through the roof, you may regret your decision.

---

last modified 7 June 2014, www.ato.gov.au/Individuals/Ind/Rental-properties---avoiding-common-mistakes/ and www.ato.gov.au/Individuals/Ind/Rental-properties---avoiding-common-mistakes/?page=4. Please note that legislation can change at any time and you should always seek independent taxation advice.

The worst thing about refinancing is that the bank still holds a mortgage over your property. Each time you refinance, you need to work with the bank or your finance broker.

In the "pay off" option, you still buy multiple investment properties, but when the properties have increased sufficiently in value, you sell one to pay off the mortgage on another.

If you choose this strategy, I recommend buying twice as many properties as you want to hold. If you ultimately want to own five investment properties debt-free, buy ten. If you would like to eventually own 10 properties, buy 20. Whatever number of properties you have in mind to hold, double it. You can buy these properties as quickly or as slowly as you like. You are the master of your plan.

Just as in Option 1 above, I suggest you buy one property a year for the next 10 years. Again, you can change this to suit your circumstances if you like.

The benefit of the "pay-off" option is your ultimate financial security and independence. You are working towards being free from banks and debt. In the end, you own the title to your investment properties, and all the rent received from those investments is yours to live on in retirement.

The importance of having a plan

As I mentioned earlier, it is important to have a clear plan in mind when you are buying your investment properties. Having a plan will take away a lot of stress and anxiety.

You don't have to pick one plan and stick to it forever. You can change your mind, or you can have a different plan for each property. But I have always bought an investment property with a specific goal in mind.

I've bought some properties for the sole purpose of making money, intending only to make cosmetic improvements and minor renovations before reselling the property to make some extra cash. I have not wanted to keep these properties indefinitely because I believed they would require too much ongoing maintenance or were not located in an area that would attract significant capital growth in the future. In these cases, I identified the property as being well below its true market value, and my interest was purely opportunistic and short-term. But while I bought, renovated and resold these properties, I also held other investment properties that I have no intention of ever selling. However, "ever" is a very long time, and I know it's important to look out for factors that might require me to reconsider my position.

The point is, even though I've invested with various motivations, *I have always purchased an investment property with a plan in mind.* Before I have signed the purchase contracts, I know whether I intend to make some quick money from the property, or would prefer to hold onto it indefinitely. My investment portfolio always includes both kinds of properties. If I change my mind and decide to keep an investment property I had intended to sell, or to sell an investment property I had intended to keep, it's okay.

The important thing is to have a clear plan in mind. Don't buy one investment property and stop, like most people do. Buy multiple properties and have a 10-year plan. If you do this, you can **retire in 10 years**.

Summary

- Always purchase an investment property with a plan in mind.
- To sell at a profit, your sale price should exceed all costs involved in acquiring your investment, capital expenditure costs, and costs involved with selling your property.

- The biggest disadvantage to selling your property is that you make a profit on it only once.
- One strategy for investors who want to buy and sell properties is flipping: buying poorly presented properties and making cosmetic improvements before reselling at a profit.
- When holding onto a property, you can consider two strategies to create income: refinancing, or paying the property off and living on the rental income.
- Refinancing involves getting a larger mortgage that replaces your existing loan. The advantage is that you can keep your property and have it generate income indefinitely; the downside is that your properties will always be mortgaged and you will have to maintain a close relationship with your bankers.
- Few investors own more than one property. By buying multiple properties, it is possible to build enough income to retire in 10 years.

2. What property should I buy?

Buying off the plan

When I started to build my investment portfolio, I began with off-the-plan properties. I did this mainly because where I live, in the state of Victoria, Australia, I enjoy considerable stamp-duty savings when I buy that kind of real estate.

As I explained in my first book, though, there can be pitfalls when purchasing off the plan. Rooms may not be as big in real life as they appeared on the plan or in promotional materials. Creative drawings might show furniture in rooms that in reality are too small to accommodate it. Rooms might seem claustrophobic because the ceiling height is lower than you expected. Or the development might not proceed due to insufficient pre-sales.

In spite of the numerous potential problems involved in buying off-the-plan properties, it is still a great way to buy if you have the right knowledge. For one thing, you absolutely must read the contract of sale carefully, or have your solicitor read it. In my experience, these contracts are typically huge and include lots of legal jargon—which makes them a mine-field.

One common clause you will find is the sunset clause, which allows the developer or purchaser to rescind the contract if the development is not built or completed within a certain time. Another clause you will typically find allows the developer to make changes to the plans or finishes after the contracts have been signed. In some instances, changes to the contracts are perfectly reasonable and necessary. Tiles selected for the kitchen might no longer be available from the manufacturer, for instance. But some changes can be made solely for the financial benefit of the developer.

Investors buying off the plan should also be very familiar with reading plans and have a clear under-standing of how big rooms are. A 3 × 3 m bedroom is not a double bedroom, and it is not suitable as a main bedroom. Similarly a 5 × 4 m lounge room is a very tight room, and would not offer space for a dining area within it.

Even the "smallest room in the house" needs to be considered. Most properties include a separate toilet, and plans will often show the door swings inward to-ward the toilet. What the plan stops short of showing is that there may not be adequate space to open the door towards you when you are standing in the room.

Most of us will have encountered a poorly built toilet like this, where you have to squeeze up against the toilet bowl so there's enough room for you to open the door and get out. If you don't have a lock on the door and someone barges in without knocking, you could even receive a knee bashing. It's obviously an unattractive feature to anyone who might be looking to live there.

So, having a clear understanding of how to read plans is essential. Anyone can learn. Start by measuring the rooms in your house, your friends' houses, or your parents' house. Look at how big their rooms are. Is there enough space? Would you make rooms larger?

As you're doing this, you will notice that the types and sizes of rooms found in houses and apartments have changed over time. Many older homes had separate dining rooms for formal entertaining. Today, we rarely see separate dining rooms, but instead a house might have a theatre room for the home-cinema experience. Many older homes had large bedrooms and by today's standards comparatively small lounge rooms. But in the 1980s and 90s, the trend was to have large, open-plan living areas. Many homes today have separate living areas for use as children's play areas.

There are many reasons why the room sizes and

types change over time. The most important thing is to understand what large rooms and small rooms look like when reading a property floor plan.

One of the great advantages of buying a property off the plan is that it is brand new. The new carpets, light fittings, window furnishings, and kitchen appliances, along with a range of other things, can all be depreciated at tax time and provide fantastic claimable deductions.

To maximise your tax savings via depreciation, it is best to use the services of a quantity surveyor, who will inspect your property, identify all items you can claim depreciation on, and provide you with a depreciation schedule that will list items including the building, floor coverings, electrical appliances, heating systems, and air-conditioning units, and the lifespan of each item.

Another advantage when buying off-the-plan properties is that being new, they are generally easier to find tenants for. Tenants love living in a brand new property. Like a new car, it smells new, everything is clean, and everything is working.

We try to hold onto that new feeling as long as we can. We take greater care with new items, make sure that we don't damage them, and clean them more often. It is the same with a new property. Tenants realise they have to take greater care with a new property because when they leave, every mark on the wall or spot on the carpet will be attributed to them. If there is any damage to the property above and beyond fair wear and tear, the tenants will be held responsible and money will be taken from the bond they paid to the estate agent before moving into the property.

A bond is usually equivalent to four weeks' rent. In certain circumstances, it can be more. A bond is held specifically for use in fixing any damage caused by a tenant, or to cover rent owed if the tenant vacates the property without giving appropriate notice. If a tenant leaves a property in a clean, undamaged condition, they are entitled to receive their bond back in full.

Because bonds can be quite a large sum of money, tenants are always keen to get their money back. It is therefore in their best interests to look after the property they live in. If the bond being held is insufficient to cover damage caused by tenants, legislation gives landlords the ability to seek further compensation, but it is highly advisable to have appropriate insurance to cover any additional expenses.

When a property is new, tenants do not have any excuses for damaging it or leaving it in an unclean state. In older, established properties, on the other hand, tenants can argue the damage was already there when they moved in.

I have also found that tenants in new properties are more likely to extend their lease beyond the initial term. This is probably because they have made a comfortable home for themselves and moving into an older property won't feel as nice as what they currently have.

Improving established properties

In some Australian states, and in many other places, there is no tax saving involved in buying off-the-plan properties, which makes them less attractive. But there remains a huge amount of choice when selecting an investment property to buy.

The most desirable investment is a property you can make money from even without factoring in capital growth. Properties that best fit this criterion are houses that have been neglected and require lots of love and updating, but not structural improvements.

Many readers will be familiar with the saying "buy the worst house in the best street," and to a degree I concur. It is desirable to buy in a good street in a good area, but the *worst* home may require too much work and expense—especially if the property requires structural work.

The perfect property to make money from needs

work like gardening, painting, and new carpets, floor coverings, window furnishings, and light fittings. You want to avoid costs for more substantial work like re-stumping, rewiring, and re-plumbing.

Of course, there are exceptions. It may make sense to do this more substantial work if you can buy the property at an extremely low price. If a property requires structural work, the building most likely does not add a lot of value to the land. In that case, you don't want to pay much more than what the land is worth.

Another exception is if you are incredibly handy and can do a lot of the necessary work yourself. Be aware, though, that wiring and plumbing should only be done by licensed professionals. If you do your own electrical work and are not licensed, you could invalidate your insurance policy. If your dwelling burns down due to faulty electrical work that you or an unlicensed electrician did, your insurance company won't cover you and you will be left with nothing but the land on which the dwelling sat.

I tend to avoid having to make structural improvements like this, as they are very expensive and the costs are not easily recouped in your sale price.

On the other hand, minor improvements like painting, carpeting, and so on make a huge and immediate difference to the appearance of a property without necessarily attracting huge expense. Without doubt, the most cost-effective improvement you can make to any property is painting. When a prospective buyer or tenant walks through a home, the first thing they notice is the paint. They don't see the condition of the wiring within the wall, the distance between the studs inside it, or whether or not there is insulation.

Initially, buyers and tenants will look through a home to see if it appeals to them, and the first impression is extremely important. Fresh paint makes a tremendous first impression, and will make a room appear bright and welcoming. The best thing about paint is that it is relatively cheap, and quick and easy to apply yourself. You don't need to employ a professional painter, but if you are going to do the work yourself, you must be patient and careful. Just as quickly as a good paint job can turn buyers or tenants on, a bad paint job that has not been cut in carefully around doorjambs, architraves, and skirting boards can turn people off. It is better not to repaint a property than to do it badly.

Just like paint, carpet and new floor coverings make an immediate and positive impression on prospective buyers or tenants. New floor coverings are a bit more expensive than paint, and so not quite as good value for money, but they come a very close second. Floor coverings make such a wonderful first impression because buyers and tenants place importance and value on these items—often more than their price warrants. People know that new floor coverings can be expensive, but if you shop around you can buy cheaper alternatives that look just as good as the expensive item.

Carpet is one thing that has become far more affordable than it was in the past. In the 1950s and 60s, carpet was considered a luxury. Many homes of that era had polished floorboards. These days, carpet is very cost-effective, can be laid quickly, and makes a massive difference to the look of a home.

Tiles have always been popular because they are so durable. They last practically forever, and better yet, are now highly fashionable. Tiles are also easy to clean.

Timber laminate is another floor covering now becoming more popular. It looks just like timber but is a fraction of the cost, resists wear, scratches, and stains, and can be easily laid and cleaned. Many of these laminate products can be clipped together, making it extremely easy to save money by laying them yourself. Increasing popularity has also made laminates much cheaper in recent years.

Other quick, easy, and cost-effective improvements include do-it-yourself (DIY) curtains and blinds, and light fittings. Most curtain and fabric shops stock ready-to-hang curtains and blinds in a full spectrum of colours and styles, which can be altered to fit almost every window size. If you are laying new flooring in a room, it makes sense to spend an extra few dollars and buy curtains or blinds to complement the new flooring.

DIY light fittings are also inexpensive and can dramatically improve the look of a home. These light fittings do not need any wiring, so you do not need an electrician to install them. I have bought trendy new light fittings, which come in all shapes and sizes, for as little as $10 each.

To get an idea of what is new and trendy, and how to put it all together, visit local display homes or look at the photos inside a home magazine. Most building companies employ interior decorators whose sole responsibility is to stay in touch with what is fashionable and what is out of vogue, and to fit out and furnish new display homes in the current style. Display homes showcase the latest in colour schemes and trends, and can be a great source of inspiration and ideas.

Undoubtedly, the best thing about the improvements I have suggested is that they are extremely cost-effective. They do not cost as much as rewiring, re-stumping, or re-plumbing, but they make a huge difference to the way the home looks. The problem with more intensive work like this is that it doesn't make a visual impact. The improvements cost a lot but the prospective buyer can't see them. If a home looks the same as when you bought it, a new buyer will expect to pay the same price you did.

Readers will have their own ideas of what is inexpensive. I consider painting, new floor coverings, curtains, blinds, and light fittings inexpensive because they increase the value of a property far more than what they cost me.

As an example, I recently bought an investment property and spent $15,000 on improvements, which included new carpet in the lounge, the three bedrooms, and the study. I also had new laminate laid in the kitchen, family room, entry, and hallway, and put new curtains in the lounge and new light fittings throughout. In the kitchen I put new door handles on the cupboards, and I had the whole home painted, inside and out. On the outside, I cleaned up the overgrown garden, removed weeds, added new garden beds, re-mulched the existing garden beds, and planted a few more shrubs.

Although I could have done some of these improvements myself and thereby saved a few dollars, I use professional tradespeople. I find it far more efficient than if I did the work myself, and the extra costs

I incur are effectively saved because I can rent out my investment property quicker and start receiving income from it sooner.

These improvements made an enormous difference to the appearance of the home, particularly the bedrooms, study, and lounge because everything you see in these rooms is new. I had the home revalued after completing the improvements, and was told that the home is worth between $40,000 and $50,000 more than I paid. Because I bought the home with the intention of retaining it as a long-term investment, I was more than happy that the rent increased by $70 per week after completing the improvements. This means that I receive an extra $3,640 rent each year. The estate agent also found a tenant very quickly because the property was well presented. Hopefully the improvements will last for 10 years, so the extra rent will well and truly cover the cost of improving my asset.

Whether you use tradespeople as I do or carry out improvements yourself to save money, doing what I have outlined above will increase the value of your property by at least the amount that it costs you. In real terms, the improvements will cost you nothing. If you sell the property, the sale price will cover the costs of the improvements, and it will be far easier to find a willing and enthusiastic buyer. If you keep the property as a rental, you will receive more rent, it will be quicker and easier to find a tenant, and that tenant will take better care of your investment.

If you are thinking of selling, making improvements is vitally important. It will save you marketing costs by reducing the time it takes to sell your property, and it will maximise the price you achieve. If you want to keep your property, the improvements help you find a tenant quicker and achieve a higher rental return. They will also increase the value of your important asset, in turn boosting your balance sheet and net wealth, which will help you if you ever wish to refinance. Also remember that at some point in the life of the property, you will have to make improvements just to maintain the standard of your asset and portfolio.

Summary

- As an investor, you will need to consider whether to buy off the plan or new properties, or established properties (or some mix of the two).
- Buying off the plan offers excellent opportunities for making tax deductions for depreciation. It is also easier to find tenants for new properties.
- When buying an established property, choose one

that requires minor renovations but not structural improvements.

- Three cost-effective improvements you can make that will increase the value of the property are painting; installing new floor coverings; and adding DIY curtains, blinds, and light fittings.
- Whether you sell or hold, making improvements will save you time and money by making it easier to find a tenant or buyer for your property.

3. Maximising your sale price

Presentation

The universal goal of every homeowner selling a property is to get the highest price possible. Estate agents can help in achieving this goal through marketing, photography, and negotiations. But sellers also need to help and play their part.

The best way to involve yourself is in presenting your property to the very best of your ability. All homeowners look at their own home through rose-coloured glasses. This is perfectly understandable: our home is our castle and we often love where we live. But when it's time to sell, we need to take an objective, unbiased look at our property.

My advice to anyone thinking about selling their home is to walk to the front of the property and look at it critically. If you find this difficult to do, it's a good idea to bring an impartial person with you for an honest opinion. If you notice any objectionable features, you can be sure that potential buyers will also see them. Put yourself in the buyer's shoes. This front view of your home is unquestionably the most important aspect. Does it look appealing, loved, cared for, and well maintained?

Front appearance

Your most important task as a seller is to persuade potential buyers standing in front of your home to walk up the driveway or path and look inside. If you can't entice buyers to look inside, you won't make a sale.

When you are looking at your home critically the things you are looking for include:

- Is the lawn mown and edged?
- Are there any weeds in the garden bed?
- Have the shrubs been pruned?
- Are there any dead plants in the garden?
- Is the letter box straight, or leaning over?
- Are the gutters clean of debris, or can you see grass growing in them?
- Can you see any peeling paint on the fascia or weatherboards?
- Are the windows clean and the curtains hanging straight?
- Are the fences straight, or leaning over?
- Are there any oil stains on the driveway?

If anything needs to be done, it should be attended to before the property is listed for sale and marketing commences. If you decide not to do the work required, prospective buyers will assume that your home is unloved and uncared for, and this make it harder to sell your property and achieve a good price.

Let's say you leave a dead plant in the garden. Buyers will think that you don't care about maintaining your home and its presentation. Removing a dead plant is only a small job, and if you can't be bothered doing a small job, what about the bigger jobs? Has the rest of the property been neglected?

I often replace the letter box at my investment properties. This small house for letters is a miniature representation of the bigger house it belongs to. Letter boxes go through trends and styles just as interior furnishings do. A dilapidated letter box that's been around as long as the Rolling Stones and is as aged as Keith Richards should be retired. A new letter box will cost a couple of hundred dollars, but will last the next 10 or more years. It's really a very small investment to make.

Similarly, new mulch in the garden beds makes a garden look fresh and well maintained.

These small improvements speak volumes about the rest of the home. How it looks outside creates an impression in the buyer's mind. If your home looks neat and tidy outside, buyers will assume that inside is similarly well cared-for. Equally, if the outside looks old, untidy, and tired, buyers will assume the worst and drive past your property without inspecting the inside.

First impressions count

You can only make a first impression once. If you don't convince buyers standing outside to come in for a look, they will not come back a second time.

As an estate agent, I have sold many homes to buyers who have fallen in love with the way a home has looked outside, even if they have strongly disliked—or even hated!—the inside. But the converse is very rare: you will almost never sell a home to a buyer who dislikes the outside but loves the inside.

A buyer will still consider purchasing a dwelling they only love the look of from the outside because they intend to change the inside to suit them so that they can proudly call their new abode "home." They will be excited about their new purchase and can't wait to give family and friends the address of their new place so that they can do a drive-by—even before they've settled and moved in.

By contrast, a buyer who dislikes the look of a

home but loves the inside will usually walk away from a property. The buyer would be embarrassed to tell family and friends the address of their new home. This may seem superficial, but we live in a superficial world. If something looks good, we usually think it is good.

Even if you live in a unit at the rear of a block, don't exempt yourself from this critical self-inspection. If the front unit in your block is untidy, it detracts from the appearance of the whole block. All the units suffer because of its poor presentation.

Prospective buyers or tenants will assume, correctly or incorrectly, that the front unit is a rental property, and if it is in poor condition they may think that the block is low-rent and occupied by an undesirable demographic. If you face this situation, you could offer to mow and edge the front unit's lawn, remove dead plants, or even re-mulch their garden beds. For approximately $100, you can buy two cubic metres of woodchips: an excellent investment if it helps with the presentation and sale of your unit.

Getting involved in the presentation of other units may seem extreme, but making a good first impression is paramount. I have on occasions mown my neighbour's front yard and nature strip when I was selling a property I owned, because I did not want the neighbour's untidy yard to have a negative impact on my sale price.

As an estate agent, I have also approached the occupants of a front unit and organised a gardener to spend a couple of hours tidying up their yard. This was necessary because if the front garden were left looking neglected and untidy, it would have unfairly diminished my client's ability to sell their unit at the back of the block for a good price. Not surprisingly, the occupants of front units have always allowed me to arrange a gardener, and sometimes they have done the work themselves to help their neighbour.

Studies conducted by researchers from New York University (NYU) have found that in the first seven seconds of meeting someone for the first time, we make eleven major decisions about them. These computations are made in lightning speed. In a similar way, we also make major decisions regarding a property we are seeing for the first time. Although I do not know how many major decisions we make in the first seven seconds, I do see potential buyers reading the front of a property the way they do a human face. I've heard buyers describing a home with its sunblinds down as a face with its eyes shut, a flat-roofed house as a face with no head, and a home with a pitched roof but no eaves looking like a face with no eyebrows.

Obviously, you can't impress every buyer, and I'm

not suggesting you put a pitched roof on your flat-roofed house, or build eaves. Beauty is in the eye of the beholder, and many buyers like flat-roofed homes, for instance. But when you have a potential buyer, you must make the most of your opportunities. After all, there are plenty of homes for sale: buyers have a huge selection to choose from. You need to make every second of that first impression count.

I am also guilty of judging books (or homes) by their covers. When I am asked to value a property, I naturally look at the outside first. Often, my first impression is, "Wow! This is a beautiful home and it will be easy to sell." But just as often, I think, "This home is going to be hard work because it looks tired and poorly presented."

At the same time, I can also be guilty of making assumptions about the owners of the home. For instance, I'll assume their age from looking at the style of their garden and the plants in it. Rocks in garden beds are now the height of fashion, along with drought-tolerant plants such as succulents and ornamental grasses and flaxes. Things like this are typically found in a younger person's garden. Traditional plants such as bush roses, hydrangeas and rhododendrons are not as popular with younger people: you'll usually find them in an older person's garden. Gardens, particularly the plants in them, are very susceptible to trends and fashions. Consider—what does your garden say about you?

Because the first impression is so vital, if you are renovating a property you should start at the front kerb and progressively work your way from the front to the back fence. But often homeowners get things the wrong way around and begin by renovating the inside of their home, and ignore the front appearance.

This is natural: we spend more time inside our home than in the front yard, which we may think is there just for the benefit of our neighbours across the road. Unfortunately, by the time they've finished renovating the inside of a home, the owners have lost interest in the project and the front never gets done. When the time comes to sell, they have a beautifully renovated interior that no one comes in to see because it is hidden behind a boring, old façade.

To avoid this happening to you, make sure you renovate the front of your home first. That way, even if you never get to the inside, you will have done the most important part of the whole job. A home with an unrenovated interior but an attractive exterior will always get more enquiries from potential buyers and tenants than one with a renovated interior but unattractive exterior.

Preparing the interior

After you have critically assessed the front appearance of your home and made necessary changes and renovations, you need to prepare the inside.

Every home has its own personality. Even if two identical homes were built side by side, after not much time has passed they will have their own history, be furnished and presented differently, and will feel different. Your home's personality is created by the colours, textures, lighting, and furnishings you use inside. It can be light and joyful or dark and brooding. You can have light or dark painted walls, heavy blackout curtains or sheer blinds, large light fittings or concealed downlights.

Our personal preferences ensure that we all furnish and present our homes' differently, but when selling, remember that you want to engage as many buyers as possible. There will always be some presentation strategies that work better than others.

I particularly recommend that you allow as much natural light inside as you can. I have never received a negative comment from a buyer about there being too much light in a home, but I have heard many negative comments about rooms and entire homes that were too dark. To improve the feeling of natural light inside your home, make sure that shrubs and trees near windows are pruned, and that windows are spotless, with no fingerprints or grime visible. If your windows have fly-screens, make sure there are no holes or tears.

When you are preparing your home for sale, start by pretending you are a potential buyer and take a self-guided tour into and all the way through your home. When you walk to the front door, is it inviting? When you step into the entry foyer, is it welcoming? Just like you did when judging the outside of your home, try to adopt a critical, unbiased view.

Living areas

Most homes are furnished when they are being sold. This is preferable, but not necessarily essential. A vacant house can still have a welcoming personality, but it must be spotlessly clean: without the distraction of furnishings, buyers will notice every imperfection and unclean surface. If your home is furnished, it should be neat, tidy, and uncluttered.

A buyer inspecting your property will usually begin in a living area. You need to make sure there are no obstructions in their way—they should be able to walk through and feel a sense of comfort and space. If necessary, consider removing furniture to make the rooms appear larger than they really are. Take down posters and remove excessive knick-knacks;

keep built-in cupboards and surface areas orderly.

A potential buyer needs to be able to imagine their furniture in your home: their lounge suite in your living room, their dining table in your meals area. If a buyer starts drawing these items on the floor plan, which you should make copies of for marketing purposes, it is usually a good sign—they are mentally moving into your home.

Don't be too ruthless in clearing furnishings and other signs of life from your living spaces. Ideally, you want to appeal to an owner-occupier rather than an investor. Someone wanting a home for themselves and their family will generally pay more. Buyers like this are emotionally attached to their decision—potentially the decision to buy *your* home —whereas an investor will make a business decision based upon cold, hard numbers. Just like you, other investors are looking for bargains that they can profitably rent out or resell.

An owner-occupier is looking for a dream: a place to live, not just a house. Therefore, you need to keep it infused with personality. Too much furniture may create a sense of clutter, disorder, or even stress, and prevent buyers from visualising their own family and furniture there. But if you go overboard with the de-cluttering, potential buyers may feel your home is cold and sterile. Remember that your home is a celebration of your life, and should express how much you love living there. Keeping a few personal items like coffee table magazines, picture frames, and note-pads on show is not just acceptable—it's desirable. Just make sure you get rid of anything that might be thought of as dirt or mess.

Kitchen

The kitchen is often referred to as the heart of the home. When presenting a property, it is *essential* that the kitchen is clean and clear of clutter. This even extends to cleaning the inside of the oven and the front of your fridge.

Professional photographers will always make sure that all magnets and sticky notes have been re-moved from the fridge before photographing the kit-chen. These items on a fridge look messy. During the sale campaign, it is best to minimise the amount of clutter on our fridge, but if we are still living in our home, it must stay comfortable and practical, so a shopping list or child's picture on the fridge is expec-ted. One or two small items like this keep the place feeling lived in.

The bench space and food preparation area sho-uld appear as large as possible, so put anything you don't need in the cupboards. Leave no dirty dishes in the sink. Buyers will often look in the pantry, so make sure it is neat and organised. Polish the sink, taps, stove and splashback, and any appliances that are normally left out, such as the kettle and toaster.

You want to give the buyer the impression that preparing a meal in your kitchen is a culinary delight. Generally, when a couple are looking through a home, the female makes the final decision. Often, the kitchen is the most important room to them, so presentation and cleanliness is of prime importance.

Smells can also influence how we think about a room, and the kitchen is one of the rooms where smells can be most evident. Different cultures usually have different foods they are accustomed to cooking: South Asians will often cook curries, Thais will use chilli, fish sauce and herbs, and many cuisines use a lot of garlic. All these foods can be very fragrant, and it is important that these smells are not overpowering.

In the kitchen, you need to pay particular attention not only to lingering cooking odours, but also smells from the rubbish bins. In the house more broadly, if you have pets or are a smoker you need to be mindful of the associated smells. These factors can greatly affect how buyers feel about your home.

As well as eliminating unpleasant smells, it is important to create pleasant ones. Use scented candles, lemon peel, fresh flowers, and fruit—all these give a home a clean, fresh scent, and heighten its appeal.

Bathroom

In the past half-century, bathrooms and en-suites have transformed dramatically, from being small, functional rooms we scarcely thought about to chic, trendy showpieces. Kitchens and bathrooms can cost a lot of money and are now highly fashionable.

Just like kitchens, bathrooms will attract female buyers' disapproval if they are not sparkling clean. Simple ways to improve their appearance is by adding candles, scented soaps, and fluffy towels. You can also make small, inexpensive improvements to your bathroom with new towel rails, light fittings, and doorknobs on the vanity unit.

If your bathroom requires a bit more attention, consider updating the vanity, adding new mirrors, and replacing old mirrors. Mirrors have become considerably more affordable in recent years, and they will make the room look larger and brighter.

There are also some fantastic paints now available that are specifically designed for use on wall tiles. Often, bathrooms seem to be trapped in the 1950s or 60s because of the tiles which were used, which may be dark in colour. High gloss white paint on these tiles will instantaneously transform a dated bathroom, making it look cleaner and more modern at the same time. Tile paint will also help hide any cracked, missing, or stained grouting.

A good, thorough clean of the bath and shower screens will also add sparkle to this important room.

Bedroom

Bedrooms are our private sanctuaries, where we escape our kids, hide from our partners when they have a job they want us to do, and recover from the stresses of life. We should make these rooms inviting enough that buyers want to sit on the end of the bed and take a moment to relax.

Make the bed. Add large pillows and a throw rug to impart a sense of luxury.

Teenagers' bedrooms will invariably have a lot of posters of sporting heroes or pop icons. This is expected and accepted, but make sure there aren't *too* many, otherwise buyers may be suspicious that they are there to hide marks and damage on the wall behind them.

Younger children will typically have a ready-to-reach supply of toys in their room, to be thrown at their siblings at a moment's notice or put to myriad other uses. This is also expected. Because your home is a celebration of your life (which includes celebrating your child's ability to throw their toys), you don't need get every toy out of sight and into the cupboards. Just make sure buyers can easily see how large the child's bedroom is, and that they can walk through comfortably without tripping over Buzz Lightyear. Make your child's bed, close the cupboard doors, and keep the floor relatively clear, and the room is ready to show.

Laundry and toilet

Even the smallest rooms in the house need to be considered. Keep the laundry and toilet clean. The washing machine lid should be down, as should the toilet seat. Cupboard doors should be closed. Remove dirty clothes from sight: since you're closing the lid, you can hide them in the washing machine! The ironing board, clothes horses, and washing hampers should be neatly stored away. Make sure any benchtops are clean and uncluttered.

Preparing the exterior

Backyard

By the time the buyer has walked through your home, they have largely made up their mind if they want to buy it or not. But you still cannot afford to totally ignore the outdoor entertaining area and back garden.

Provided the back garden looks respectable and is of a suitable size, it won't change the buyer's mind if they have already decided they'd like to buy. For this reason, the back garden does not need the same meticulous attention that the front required. But you must present a neat, tidy yard.

Make sure the lawn is mown and the edges trimmed. Remove dead plants as you did in the front; you may also need to put new woodchips in the garden beds.

The most important feature of the back garden to any buyer is the size, and that, obviously, is very difficult to change. Provided the yard is big enough, a buyer can re-landscape and transform it if they like. Most buyers will have their own preferences in plants and landscaping, and in my experience, they usually change a back garden to fit their own image of what the great outdoors should look like.

Because personal preference is such a big factor in gardening, I do not recommend that you spend a lot of money in the backyard, particularly on plants, which can be very expensive. The most important thing is just that your garden is neat and well presented. Ideally, it should also look relatively easy to care for and maintain.

If you need to add some interest and a splash of colour to your garden, an easy way is to add some pots with flowering plants. The best thing about pots is that you can take them with you when you sell your home.

Sheds

I have on many occasions sold homes where the garage or shed has been full to the rafters with household treasures—or rubbish, depending on your point of view. This is perfectly acceptable. Unlike your home, the garage and shed are allowed to be cluttered. If a couple is looking through your home, often only the male will be interested in the sheds. The crucial information he needs is: does the garage or shed have power? Does it have a concrete or a dirt floor? Is it waterproof? If a shed or garage is packed full of items, that's a good sign—it is very likely weatherproof.

Getting ready to sell

After critically self-assessing your property, and investing your energy and effort in tidying up and making improvements, it's time to get a return on your hard work by making some money.

The improvements should be evident. You've attended to all minor imperfections and repairs. Finally, make sure the carpet and floor tiles are clean and ready for inspection. Professional cleaning can make an amazing difference.

In a highly competitive market such as real estate, it is important to create an emotional bond between the buyer and your property. Even investors must become emotionally attached to your property to some extent before they will buy it. Creating a welcoming environment that appeals to buyers' wants and needs will give you a greater chance of achieving an outstanding price. As I have mentioned, the appearance of your home, the amount of natural light there, and even the way it smells all create an impression.

One last consideration is sound. So that your home does not seem stuffy and sterile to buyers, consider playing some soft background music in the right genre. Retailers have been doing this for years. It has been proven that light classical music can be used to great effect, making buyers stay longer and increasing the chances of a sale.

By creating the right environment in your home, you will increase the number of buyers interested in your property.

Pricing

Setting the correct price for a property when listing it for sale will always be one of the hardest and most important challenges for owners and estate agents. The estate agent faces the dilemma of wanting to list the property at a low price to achieve a quick sale, while also knowing that the overwhelming majority of property owners have an overinflated opinion of their own properties' value.

When estate agents are asked to value a property, they will often give a generous or optimistic price estimate so that they do not offend the owner and give themselves the best chance of listing the property for sale. This is particularly true when the agent knows that they will be in competition with other agents for the owner's business. To win the owner's confidence, all the competing agents are likely to give the owner a generous estimate of the property's true value.

In addition to receiving typically generous estimates of their property's value, owners compound the problem by adding a negotiating buffer above the agent's price estimate. Their greatest fear is underselling their property.

Because of these factors, most properties are initially listed at too high a price, in some cases tens of thousands of dollars above where they should be if they are to attract buyer interest. After a fruitless marketing campaign and buyer inspections, the owners receive a reality check and become aware of the error.

If that happens to you, by the time the price is reduced to the correct level, buyers in the area have moved onto the next new listing, and the hype and excitement surrounding your property has dissipated. Buyer inspections and enquiries for your property become fewer, and achieving a sale seems a more and more distant prospect.

As a seller, you are now relying upon new buyers entering the market. The existing pool of qualified buyers has been exhausted. Many of these have now bought elsewhere. In some instances, a qualified buyer who looked at the property when it was first listed may reconsider your property when the price has been reduced. If they do make an offer, such a buyer will at this point be harder to negotiate with, because they believe they have an advantage over the seller.

The buyer will argue that the property has not sold because it is still too expensive and has limited appeal. They will also claim that the owner, who is becoming increasingly desperate, should be grateful for their offer, which they should accept to avoid the property sitting on the market for an extended period with no interest, all the while incurring costly, ongoing marketing expenses.

You want to avoid this downward spiral. So, as a property owner, what should you do?

You should not ignore the price given to you by the agent, but be aware that the agent's price may be a little high, particularly when the property is initially listed. If the price is high, it is pointless admonishing the agent and laying all blame on them, because property owners can carry out their own market research on prices and often choose agents who gave them a higher valuation over those who were more conservative with their price estimates.

Listing your property for sale at the correct price from the outset is of paramount importance. When you first list your property for sale, it is new and exciting; there are buyers who are ready and waiting to buy your property *right now*. These buyers have done their research and inspected enough properties in preceding months that they are confident in their own estimates of a property's value, and are ready to make offers. They have organised their finance, perhaps offered on other properties and missed out, or were the under bidder at an auction.

Estate agents consider these buyers to be A-class: they are ready to buy the right property at the right price, as soon as they find it. Any new listing is high on their priority list to view, and agents they are in contact with will notify them whenever a potentially suitable property comes onto the market. These buyers have probably also registered for internet alerts that will automatically email the buyer when new properties matching their search criteria appear on major real-estate sites.

If your property is listed at the correct price, neither overinflated nor undervalued, it will create interest and competition and you will achieve a sale.

There are three ways to make sure that you list your property at the correct price. They are:

1. Do your own research

Just as you would carry out due diligence before buying a property, use the same methodology and ensure you are getting the best result possible for your property.

The key points to remember when you are carrying out your research are:

- Only reference properties that have sold in close proximity to your property (say 3–4 kilometres).
- Only reference properties that have sold in the last six months. Properties that are still for sale

are irrelevant, because they could sell for significantly less than the asking price, and more importantly some of them have such inflated asking prices that they never sell and are later withdrawn from the market.

- Properties for comparison should appeal to the same group of buyers as your own (e.g. family home buyers, first home buyers, etc.).

- Comparable properties should offer the same number of bedrooms, and similarly sized living spaces and land. They should be about the same age (or have been renovated to bring the property up to date) and their construction should be the same (e.g. both brick, both timber, etc.).

- Finally, compare only apples with apples. There is no benefit in comparing homes with units, townhouses, flats, or villas. They appeal to different buyers and can achieve vastly different sales results.

For further information about carrying out due diligence refer to the heading "Setting expectations" in Chapter 1 of my book *How to Buy Unlimited Investment Properties.*

2. Use a sworn valuer

Employ an independent sworn valuer to carry out a market valuation. Unlike an estate agent, the valuer is not competing for your business, so they do not need to inflate the valuation figure just to make you happy. They will get paid whether your property sells or not.

If you choose this option, make sure that you tell the valuer that you want a market valuation and intend to sell your property. Property owners have often informed me that they have a valuation carried out by their bank some time ago for refinancing purposes, or to see how much money they could borrow for their next home. A valuation done for this purpose is often not as accurate as a market valuation: it can be manipulated, to a degree, to fulfil certain objectives—e.g. to demonstrate equity growth in a property and secure a larger loan for your next investment.

As a seller, you want a true indication of what your property is worth today. The best way to find this out is by getting a current market valuation using comparative sales results.

3. List your property for sale without a price

You can do this by using an auction, tender, or set sale (also called *sale by set date*), giving the price on application, or using a similar marketing strategy. Each strategy has an extensive list of pros and cons, and you could write a book just on the merits of each one.

～

The strategy you employ should be tailored to suit your particular property, its location, and the market conditions at the time. In my opinion, there is no one best strategy for everyone. Many estate agents hold a different view, but those views are often coloured by their personal preferences and what *they* want to achieve for themselves, which may differ from what is best for the property and the owner.

As I have mentioned, it is crucial that a property is listed at the correct price from the outset.

A survey conducted in relation to the Pilling System for marketing real estate best illustrates the reason why this is so important. In this study, 141 homes were independently valued just before being listed for sale. The study recorded the correlation between sale price and days on the market. When a property was sold, the sale price was compared with the independent valuation and the difference between the two was recorded as a percentage above or below the valuation figure. The time needed to sell the property was also recorded. The results of this study are shown below in Figure 1.

Figure 1: The relationship between valuation accuracy and time on the market.

The results show that in the first 2–2.5 weeks after listing a property for sale, the owners are more likely to sell their property above the independent valuation figure. After 2–2.5 weeks, the chances of selling a property above the valuation steadily declines. Once a property has been on the market for 46 days or longer, the owners are more likely to achieve a sale price *less* than the valuation figure.

The results clearly show that to get the best price for your property, it is best to sell before it sits too long on the market and becomes stale. A quicker sale is also preferable, because you will spend less money on marketing and it is less stressful for the owner.

Commission

If an estate agent persuades you to list your property with them because they are confident that they can achieve a sale price above your expectations and those of the other agents, make sure the agent is held accountable. The best way to do this is by making sure the agent puts their money where their mouth is.

An estate agent will only get paid if they sell your property. Their payment is called *commission*. Typically, an estate agent's commission is calculated as a flat percentage fee of the sale price. The percentage fee is usually 2–3%, and is negotiable.

Usually, the more expensive the property is, the larger the commission fee will be, even though the actual commission rate may be lower when expressed as a percentage. As an example, a typical commission fee for a property valued at $300,000 is 3%, which equates to $9,000. The typical commission fee for a property worth $1 million is only 1.5%, but this comes to $15,000.

To ensure that an estate agent puts their money where their mouth is, negotiate a *tiered commission.*

A tiered commission has two or more percentage rates. If an estate agent is confident that they can achieve a certain price, then hold them accountable by structuring a tiered commission rate around the agent's price expectation. The best way to do this is offer the agent a lower than normal commission rate up to a figure that you consider reasonable and then give the agent an incentive to meet their price expectations and yours by including a bonus commission rate for any amount they achieve above your nominated figure.

For instance, let's say an estate agent says they can sell your property for $550,000 but you believe it is only worth around $500,000, you can offer a tiered commission rate that pays the agent 1.5% of the sale price up to $500,000, plus a 50% bonus on the amount that exceeds $500,000. If the agent genuinely thinks that they can achieve a sale price above $500,000, they will be excited by this commission structure and be correctly incentivised to work hard to get you the best price possible. In this example, the agent receives $7,500 commission at a sale price of $500,000, but $32,500 if they can sell the property for $550,000.

If the agent squirms and starts making excuses about why they cannot accept your tiered commission, you know they don't truly believe that they can achieve the price they have given you. The agent has inflated the expected sale price to buy your confidence and your listing.

An agent like this will use excuses such as, "the base commission rate of 1.5% is too low and our company policy prohibits us from accepting tiered commissions." Excuses like this are false: all estate agents will negotiate their commission, and will accept a tiered commission if the bonus offers more than their usual compensation and they believe that the necessary price is achievable. The estate agent will typically argue against a tiered commission only if they do not believe that they can reach the bonus level you have set on the basis of an inflated price they themselves have offered you.

An example is provided in Table 2 of a typical commission rate versus a tiered commission rate for a property worth around $500,000:

Many sellers will look straight at the bottom line, compare a $13,500 commission to a $27,500 commission, and be aghast that the tiered commission rate can end up costing twice as much as the typical commission rate.

This is true: the tiered commission could cost

Sale price	Typical commission*	Tiered commission†
$460,000	$11,500	$6,900
$470,000	$11,750	$7,050
$480,000	$12,000	$7,200
$490,000	$12,250	$7,350
$500,000	$12,500	$7,500
$510,000	$12,750	$7,500 + $5,000 = $12,500
$520,000	$13,000	$7,500 + $10,000 = $17,500
$530,000	$13,250	$7,500 + $15,000 = $22,500
$540,000	$13,500	$7,500 + $20,000 = $27,500

* 2.5% † 1.5% to $500K plus 50% of amount above $500K

Table 2: Commission rate comparison

more. But if it does, you still end up with more money in your pocket than if the property had fetched a lower price. Your focus should remain on the two most important issues: "What is my property worth?" and, "How do I get the best price?"

If you correctly believed your property was worth $500,000 and it sells for that, under the tiered commission structure you will only pay the agent $7,500, saving you $5,000. Likewise, if the agent gives you an inflated price estimate and they sell the property for less, they will miss out on commission. This ensures that they must estimate the price as accurately as possible when they are appraising your property.

In this scenario, if you are lucky enough to sell your property for $540,000, which is $40,000 above your expected price, it will cost you an extra $14,000 in commission fees, *but you keep the remaining $26,000.*

The problem with the typical commission structure is that a $10,000 difference in sale price only adds or removes $250 from the agent's commission. This does not give the agent a strong enough incentive to go the extra distance to get you the best price. If your own price estimate is $500,000 and your agent truly believes that they can do better, reward them if they are correct. Remember, if they are right, you *both* share in the bonus. Under the tiered commission structure as I described it, the estate agent receives an extra $5,000 for every $10,000 increase they achieve above $500,000. This is obviously far more attractive to the agent than receiving an extra $250 for every $10,000 more they get on the sale price. As a result, the tiered commission structure correctly incentivises the agent to get you the best price possible.[4]

_____

[4]Remember that commission rates are negotiable; the above is just an example. Commission rates and structures are usually negotiated with the agent at the time of listing your property for sale. When you discuss commission rates with the agent, you may negotiate different rates than I have shown above. If you do negotiate a higher base rate, make sure that the bonus rate is lowered accordingly. Put simply, the lower the base rate

Beware: if you are negotiating a tiered commission rate, use only a bonus level as described above, not a variable commission rate for different price targets *that applies to the whole of the sale price.* A variable commission rate like this is where you pay, for instance, 1.5% up to $500,000 ($7,500 on $500,000), and a second rate of 3% if the property sells for above $500,000 ($15,150 on $505,000).

This may appear to offer an adequate incentive to the agent, but it has inherent problems. On the surface, it may seem logical and fair. If the estate agent cannot achieve the price of $500,000, they receive a reduced commission. But if they do achieve a sale price over $500,000, they are adequately rewarded, with a commission rate above the typical rate of 2.5%. The major problems are that once the estate agent reaches the bonus level there is not enough incentive to keep them pushing for the highest price, and if the sale price just tips over the bonus level the cost to the seller can outweigh the benefit.

The example in Table 3 illustrates the potential hazards with using this structure.

The problem with this structure is clearly evident when the agent gets just over $500,000. If the property sells for $499,000, the commission payable is $7,485, but if the property sells for just $2,000 more

---

is, the higher you can afford to make the bonus rate.

Sale price	Commission*
$460,000	$6,900
$470,000	$7,050
$480,000	$7,200
$490,000	$7,350
$500,000	$7,500
$510,000	$15,300
$520,000	$15,600
$530,000	$15,900
$540,000	$16,200

*1.5% up to $500K, or 3% if over $500K

Table 3: Hazards of applying a variable commission rate to the entire sale price

($501,000), the commission payable jumps to $15,030. For achieving an extra $2,000 on your sale contract you will pay the agent an extra $7,545, *losing $5,545.* You can see why this commission structure should be avoided at all costs.

Advertise

There are two truths about real-estate marketing.

1. You cannot sell a secret
2. Real estate is a numbers game.

There will always be exceptions, where a property is just listed and even before photos can be taken and advertisements drafted, the property sells for a great price and the neighbours wonder what happened.

But most sellers are not the exception. You will need to work a bit harder and smarter than you might have expected to realise that fantastic sales result you hope for. That means you need to tell as many people as possible that your property is for sale. The best way to do this is to *advertise.*

When it comes to promoting your property, there are now numerous choices available for sellers. Many of them didn't exist in the past.

Traditionally, when you listed your property for sale the agent would place an advertisement in the major local newspaper, put a photo and description in their office window, and erect a "for sale" board at the front of your property. In those days, hopeful buyers would visit the estate agent's office, jump in the back of the agent's car, and be chauffeured around to look at listings. Buyers and estate agents would get to know one another and build a relationship.

In today's fast-paced society, expectant buyers want all the information immediately, at the push of a button. There is no need to visit an estate agency, and you wouldn't dream of hopping in the back of an agent's car to be driven around the neighbourhood. To sate the buyers' appetite for information, new advertising media and services are regularly being developed. Now you may be offered services including virtual tours, QR codes, video, 3D or interactive floor plans, copywriting, professional photography, graphic design, Photoshopping, home stylists, and advertising on new websites, including social media platforms.

All of these new developments and options make it increasingly difficult and confusing to know where to get the best result from marketing. Because so much information is now readily available to prospective buyers, the rapport that estate agents had with buyers has slowly eroded and, unfortunately, so has much of the trust that buyers used to place in their estate agent.

Whilst the explosion of marketing options has made it increasingly difficult to know where to place your ads, it has also made it more important to advertise. This is the only reliable way that buyers will see your property is for sale. You can no longer rely on the estate agent alone to find you the perfect buyer: you need to help by advertising.

This certainly does not mean that you have to advertise everywhere, or that you need an unlimited advertising budget. Advertising can be very expensive, and you do not need to agree to every advertising option the estate agent presents to you. Advertisements need to be carefully planned and targeted to ensure that you get the best result, which means reaching the largest possible audience for your property.

Because every area, suburb, town, and neighbourhood is different, and different newspapers operate in those areas, it is impossible for me to recommend, in this book, one advertising campaign that would perfectly suit every property. The estate agent is the best person to give things like the size, content, and frequency of the ads you place, and where you should place them.

The fundamental aim of any advertising campaign is to reach as many buyers as possible. As I have mentioned, advertising has evolved significantly over the years. During this time, newspaper classifieds' dominance in property advertising has fallen, and the internet has risen in importance, but neither medium will reach all buyers. As a result, you now need to consider advertising in newspapers *and* online.

The chances of a buyer finding your property from the board at the front of your property, the estate agent's office window, or a letter-box drop have always been remote. Each of these methods is usually responsible for finding the buyer for a property on only around 6% of occasions, as we discovered from research at one of the estate agencies I worked at. For this reason, some sellers have argued against having a "for sale" board at the front of their property. But your property could be one of the 6% of properties sold using this form of advertising. A "for sale" board is a relatively cheap way of having an estate agent sitting at the front of your property 24/7.

If you don't use every advertising option available to you, you will never know what you have missed out on. As I have mentioned, I am not advocating reckless spending on advertising, but you need to attract as many potential buyers as possible to your property in order to achieve the best price possible. Also, when you have sold your property you want to be satisfied that you have done everything you could to achieve the best price. That means presenting and promoting your property to the very best of your ability.

If your property is promoted, priced, and presented correctly, it should sell, and for an excellent price, but you can never forget the importance of getting as many buyers as possible through the door to look at your property. Real estate is a numbers game: the more people look, the more chances you have to sell, and at a price that meets your objectives. This is why you don't want to keep the sale of your property a secret.

The numbers game: conversion rates from inspection to sale

On average, an estate agent will receive one offer for every 15 to 20 inspections through a particular property. If the agent is only showing a few buyers through your home each month, it will likely take you a very long time to sell.

To avoid this, you need to make skilful choices about advertising (promotion) and price. In the beginning, it is too early to tell if the presentation of your property is a problem: buyers have not seen it to make any judgments.

When you list your property for sale, the aim should be to get 50 or more buyer inspections through your property in the first 30 to 60 days after listing. From these 50 plus inspections, you will normally have four or five buyers re-inspect.

It is very rare that a buyer will purchase a property after only one inspection, and re-inspections are a crucial indication of how your marketing campaign is going. *Each time you have a re-inspection you are closer to making a sale.* If you have had 50 groups of buyers inspect your property but no re-inspections, you know the marketing is working, but the price, the presentation, or both have missed the mark.

If you are having plenty of inspections but no re-inspections, *you must immediately address and rectify the issues with presentation or price before the promotion loses its impact and the buyers stop coming.* From four or five buyers who have re-inspected, you will typically get three making offers. Of these buyers, one will be off the pace and their offer will be too low. This leaves the remaining two buyers to fight it out until one wins.

This a general outline of what you should hope to achieve from a typical advertising campaign. Different areas and markets will determine the numbers involved and the outcome you achieve. But if you can create results similar to what I have described above, with 50 to 60 inspections in the first month on the basis of your promotion, in cooperation with the right estate agent you will achieve a fantastic sale price for your property.

Open for inspection

Undoubtedly the best, most effective and efficient way of showing prospective buyers through your property is by using advertised "home opens" or "open for inspections".

Some sellers are very private people and do not like or even fear having their property open to the public. Knowing this, some real-estate agencies promote themselves as being against home opens to cater specifically to this group of sellers. These agencies only do this to give themselves a point of difference from other competing real-estate offices. To help them win sellers' confidence and business, they feed their fear of home opens.

Whenever I am trying to sell a property, I never spend money on advertising without a home open. I realise that this may be shocking to some sellers, but home opens definitely help sell your property quicker and for a higher price.

Why? Buying a property is a huge financial commitment for buyers, and when they are making such a big commitment, it is natural to become nervous and apprehensive. Often they will second guess themselves and question whether they are doing the right thing. They ask themselves questions like, "have I done enough research?", "have I looked at enough properties?", and "have I paid too much?"

This is normal human behaviour. The vast majority of people will experience some self-doubt when making any number of life-changing decisions. In real estate, the feeling of regretting a purchase is called *buyer's remorse*. When buyers experience this, their normal reaction is to try and slow things down. This leads to procrastination, which drives sellers and estate agents to despair.

The seller just wants to sell. They don't want to hear the buyer's excuses about how they want to wait a bit longer before making an offer because they are suddenly experiencing doubt. But be aware that as frustrating as this is for the seller and estate agent, the buyer is being driven by a normal self-preservation instinct. The vast majority of buyers experience doubt at some stage during the buying process.

To overcome buyers' procrastination, you must create a sense of urgency and desire for them.

If you take something away from someone, or

threaten to take it away, they want it even more. Competition puts this dynamic into play. Instinctively, everyone wants to win a competition, even if they say they don't or act indifferently. Auctions work by feeding on people's competitive instincts. But even if you are not selling by auction, you can still create a competitive environment that stops buyers from procrastinating. The best way to do this is show multiple buyers through a property at the same time.

If you show a group of buyers a property and one buyer in that group likes the property, they view the other buyers present as competitors. The buyer who likes the property will transfer their feelings about it onto the others, thinking, "if I like this property, surely the others must also like it." Whether or not that is true, the interested buyer will become paranoid that others will make an offer for the property and drive the price up or cause them to miss out. The interested buyer will eavesdrop on comments made by the other buyers, and secretly, they will want the others to leave the property.

This may seem over-dramatised, but the fear of loss really drives us to act in this way. If a choice is about to be removed, you will make a decision. If there is no fear of loss, you will naturally take your time, ponder the decision, and look at every alternative.

This is true regardless of what you are buying. I recently experienced the same feelings when I bought a car. After test-driving it, I pretended to the salesperson that I was only moderately interested, and when I made an offer and negotiated the price, I tried to give the impression that I was prepared to walk away and let the car go. I thought I was succeeding, but then another salesperson walked into the office and asked for the keys so they could take another potential buyer for a drive. I folded like a deck of cards, and the negotiations ended in a flurry. Despite knowing exactly how the psychology of sales works in these scenarios and trying to use that to my advantage, I secretly wanted that car and did not want to be beaten.

Whether it is a car, a property, or a puppy in the pet-shop window, if you like it and want it, you will assume that others do too. We believe that everyone shares our taste. Rationally, we know this is not true, but when you are selling you do not want to deal with the rational buyer—you want to deal with their impulsive alter-ego, who will act decisively and pay top price to beat the competition.

You may already have put two and two together here: *home opens are so powerful because they are the most convenient way to show multiple buyers through your property at the same time.*

The other good news about home opens is that they are convenient and easy for the seller and can save you a lot of time. You can prepare in advance for the home open and ensure that your home is presented at its best, and there will not be as much need to keep your home tidy for private inspections.

Buyers prefer home opens, too, because they don't need to make a specific arrangement with the estate agent to inspect. They can simply look through at the advertised time. More importantly for the buyer, if the property is not suitable they can quickly look through and leave without feeling like they have offended the estate agent.

Property buyers also consider the weekend, particularly Saturdays, as real-estate time. They think this way because the vast majority of home opens and auctions are scheduled on Saturday so buyers can plan their weekend, do their market research, and aim to get through as many properties as possible.

Remember that real estate is a numbers game. On average, you need between 15 and 20 inspections for one offer, and in the same way, buyers need to see 15 to 20 properties before they are comfortable making an offer. Home opens allow you to get the number of buyer inspections you need quickly and efficiently. Opens also create an environment that is more conducive for competition, which will stop buyers from procrastinating and encourage them to offer a higher price.

Choosing an agent

Competition between individual real-estate agents is fierce, between agents from different agencies as well as within the same agency. Everyone wants to beat others and be the best. This is wonderful for sellers, because that competition has made professional standards improve dramatically over the years.

This is no more evident than in the market appraisal reports prepared for would-be sellers. These reports are now glossy, bound publications with photos, graphs, plans, and extensive sales information. To stay ahead of their competitors or at least keep up with them, estate agencies now consider these polished reports to be a minimum standard.

Likewise, to remain competitive, each agency provides its sales team with regular training. Real-estate industry bodies also provide extensive, ongoing training. Every estate agent's office has weekly sales meetings, training including role-play, and the latest internet tools to keep track of sales results. Each agent carries a mobile phone, is well-groomed, wears a suit, drives a late-model car, is polite, and can talk until it feels like your head will implode.

Because so much training is provided at an industry level, and because so many agents change real-estate firms bringing with them habits, procedures, and knowledge from their previous employer, it can appear that all agents are clones wearing the same Hugo Boss suit. It can be very difficult to tell them apart, and even more difficult to choose one agent to sell your property. Often the choice comes down to a hunch, nothing more than a gut feeling about who you think will be the right person for the job.

Unquestionably, the estate agent you choose should be someone you like and have some rapport with. You will be working closely with this person, have regular conversations with them, and most importantly you should be able to trust them. You will be able to find most of these important characteristics in most agents.

I believe that every agent will be able to sell your property, and every one of them will be able to get you 95–100% of what your property is worth. However, the best agents will be able to get you 5–10% more, because they have superior negotiation skills.

Even if you choose to sell your property with a pimply-faced kid straight out of school who includes a LOL or OMG in every sentence, has a diploma in

PlayStation, a tongue piercing, and no previous sales experience—you will still get 95–100% of what your property is worth. This is because when a buyer finds a property they want to buy, nothing will stop them.

The first 95–100% of the property value is not in dispute. Any reasonable buyer will accept the property's value and understand that they need to make an offer in that range to secure it for themselves. What happens after this is what distinguishes a bad estate agent from a good or great estate agent.

A **bad or lazy agent** will get an offer from the buyer, submit it to the seller, and work on convincing the seller to accept it.

A **good agent** will receive the offer, communicate it to the seller, *and then* work on the buyer to make sure that they have extracted every last dollar they can from them. They will do this regardless of whether or not the offer made is already at an acceptable level.

So, how do you find the estate agent and real-estate agency that will get you the best price?

First, you need to consider which real-estate agencies you want to invite to your property to give you their complimentary market appraisal.

Agencies not to choose

Generally, you do not want the estate agency with the lowest commissions or fees. These will tend to have the highest turnover of sales staff, which means that will likely end up dealing with an inexperienced agent. Once an agent has done their apprenticeship at one of these cheaper agencies, they usually leave and go to company where they can earn better commissions. Cheap agencies also tend to have poorer-quality marketing, and though they may sell plenty of properties, their priority is sales *volume*. They don't care that much about getting you the best price because their commission is not significantly affected if they sell the property for less than they could have. They just want as many sales as possible.

Even worse are agencies with a fixed or capped commission structure. These agencies have absolutely no monetary incentive to get the seller more money or work hard.

You also do not want the most expensive real-estate agency with the biggest ads and most ostentatious office building. These agencies look great, but all that flashiness comes at a price, and ultimately it is the seller who pays. These flashy agencies are very good at getting *vendor-paid advertising* (VPA). Their staff have a lot of training on how to convince sellers to pay for VPA, and place such high importance on it that they give out awards and incentives to agents that can bring in the most. These agencies mainly want you to use VPA not because it benefits you, but because it benefits *them*—it builds consumer awareness of their brand, and the agency's profile, which in turn attracts more listings.

The agency you should *choose*

Ideally, the estate agency you choose will already have similar properties to yours listed for sale. This means that they have a ready supply of buyers looking for your type of property in the appropriate price bracket. Their marketing will be professional and high-quality, showing that they take care and pride in presenting themselves and the sellers and properties they represent. It also shows that while they can attract VPA, they have a balanced view of how much is required to get the best result for the seller without overspending.

Finally, the agency you want will not just have similar properties to yours listed, but will also have a proven track record of selling them. You can check this by searching a real-estate directory on the internet. One of Australia's main real-estate sites, realestate.com.au, lets you view sold properties and filter them by postcode or by the agency that listed them. Similar sites around the world typically have this facility. You can also ask the estate agent for a list of similar properties they have recently sold, along with their testimonials from past clients.

Inviting two or three real-estate agencies to appraise your property for sale should be enough to gauge what your property is worth and who is the best agent for the job. As I have mentioned, be aware that when you initially list your property for sale, agents' price estimates may be a bit high because they are competing for your business and they may be trying to offer an optimistic view. To help you avoid overpricing your property, which can be a potentially fatal problem, I suggest you take the average price of the two or three appraisals you get, and use this figure to form a realistic price expectation.

Choosing the person to look after the sale of your property, who will ultimately be responsible for its sale, is the next and most important task.

Once an estate agent has your signed authority appointing them to sell your property, most of their work becomes largely automated. The signed authority is given to administrative staff back in the agency's office, where a file is created for your account. Staff will book copywriters, photographers, and graphic artists, generating a whirlwind of activity. When the marketing collateral has been prepared, the agent will present it to you, the seller, for your approval.

After that, the agent just needs to answer their phone and make times to show prospective buyers through your property. If, as the seller, you have done your part and presented the property correctly, it will eventually sell regardless of who the agent is.

Your choice of agent can, however, make a huge difference in the price you achieve. It all comes down to their negotiation skills. A skilful agent will be able to negotiate a better price. The difference could be 5–10% of the total, but depending on the value of your property this could be tens or even hundreds of thousands of dollars, and will cover the cost of the estate agent's commission with money to spare.

As I have mentioned, in a sales negotiation the first 95–100% of your property's value is not in dispute. If you have a reasonable buyer who genuinely wants to buy your property, you will get this without working too hard for it. Any estate agent, or even any vendor selling their property privately, can achieve this. Often, a buyer's opening offer will cover 95% of the eventual selling price. The question is whether you are satisfied with that outcome.

As the seller, you want to ensure that you extract the highest possible price from the buyer. Generally, this will be easier for an estate agent than for the owner trying to sell their property privately. This is because, by virtue of all their training and skills acquired on the job, the estate agent should be a better negotiator than the average seller. Buyers also know that owners trying to sell privately are not paying an agent's commission, and want this saving passed on to them in the form of a lower purchase price. Finally, information is one of the cornerstones of good negotiation: the party with more information about the other, and about the market, has an advantage. The estate agent should be more skilled than the seller at getting information out of the buyer, and out of the market.

When an estate agent meets a prospective buyer for the first time, the first thing the agent wants to know is what price bracket the buyer is looking in. Often buyers will talk their price bracket up so they are shown better properties. The agent will then establish when the buyer wants to buy. This is to determine if the buyer is an A-class buyer and ready to buy immediately, or whether they are still doing their research.

The agent will ask questions like, "have you made offers on any properties?", "have you bid at auction?", "have you organised your finance?", and "do you need to sell a property before you buy?" This information can be used against the buyer at a later stage during any negotiations. If the buyer makes an offer that is lower than one they made on another property, the agent will know that the buyer could pay more. The agent can also use the sales results of other properties the buyer has previously looked at to get an increased offer from the buyer.

When an owner is trying to sell privately, they are not privy to all this information about a prospective buyer. When a buyer is talking directly with the seller, they will undersell themselves and say things like, "I cannot afford to pay your price", "my budget won't stretch that far", "the bank has given me finance approval but at a lower price", and "I have seen better-value properties in your neighbourhood".

As I highlighted in a discussion of negotiating with valuers in chapter 1 of *How to Buy Unlimited Investment Properties*, in negotiations it is important to have more information than the opposing side. When a good estate agent is negotiating, they will give away a little information to a buyer but only in exchange for more information. As an example, during a negotiation a buyer will often be able to list all the cheaper properties that have sold in the area—so the agent needs to counter with a greater number of properties that have sold for a higher price.

When selling my own properties I have always used an estate agent, because I know if a buyer realises I am the owner, they will withhold information and I will have an entirely different conversation with them than the agent would.

As an estate agent myself, I *could* try to ignore the fact that I own the property and pretend I am selling it for a client. But the purchaser will eventually discover that I own the property: my name will appear in numerous places in the sales documentation and contracts, and I will need to sign the paperwork. When the buyer discovers this, they will rightly feel that I have been less than honest with them and withheld important information. They will also believe that I have deliberately misled them to get a higher price. Any trust that existed between us will be irrevocably lost.

Quite simply, owners are capable of selling their own properties, but a good estate agent will always get a higher price. Buyers expect that they need to pay a higher price when an estate agent is involved.

The goal for any estate agent should be to get the absolute best price they can from the buyer, regardless of whether or not it is already acceptable to the seller. This means that the estate agent has to ask the buyer again and again if they are prepared to pay more for the property. Most agencies have training called "scripts and dialogues" to teach agents what questions to ask and how, without offending the buyer and losing them. Some agents are naturally good at this, while others just think they are good. You need to find the ones who are really skilled, because that skill will more than pay for their services, putting extra money in your pocket.

More about good and bad agents

When you work in an estate agency, it is easy to tell the good agents from the poor ones. The good agents are always thinking of what they can say next to a buyer to get them to increase their offer. This is commonly referred to as "bumping." They will bump the buyer multiple times, without losing the sale, until they are absolutely satisfied they have every last cent they can get from them.

The poor agent wants the property sold as soon as possible so they can move onto the next listing.

Good agents stay in regular contact with their clients. Poor agents become quickly discouraged when a listing does not sell, and stop communicating with their client regularly.

A good agent will not blame the seller when a negotiation fails. A bad agent will.

I acknowledge that spotting the difference between a good and bad agent is very difficult for a seller. The persona that an estate agent displays to sellers can be very different from the picture you would have if you saw what went on inside their office. Naturally, if you are thinking of selling a property, you want the agent that is going to work hardest for you and will get you the best price.

Questions to ask your estate agent

When choosing your estate agent, you should be looking for the one with the best negotiation skills. To help you identify the good agents, below I have provided some questions for you to ask agents before choosing them and listing your property for sale.

1. Who will be responsible for handling all the buyer enquiries on my property? (You need to establish this, because often a senior estate agent or manager will appraise your property but its day-to-day management will be given to a PA or junior agent).

2. Who will handle the negotiations?

3. How do you make sure that you are getting the best price from the buyer?

4. What do you do if you have more than one buyer offering at the same time?

5. What price will you quote buyers? (This is particularly important if you are not disclosing a

for-sale price to the public, instead using an auction, tender, or similar system.)

6. How do you handle difficult buyers and negotiations?

7. What do you say to buyers when they ask "what is the lowest price the owners will accept?" (Every interested buyer will ask this question.)

8. Can we negotiate a lower commission fee?

When you think you have chosen your preferred agent, ask them that last question—if they will lower their commission. If they readily agree, you have chosen the wrong agent. If the agent cannot negotiate a satisfactory commission fee for themselves, they cannot negotiate an extra few thousand dollars for you on your sale price. Keep in mind that you are trying to test the agents to find out who is the best negotiator. You do not have to necessarily drive the commission rate down, you want to see who handles pressure the best.

When you appoint your agent, make sure that you only give them an authority for 60 days. This length of time should be sufficient to sell your property, or at the very least find buyers who are willing to make offers. If you are selling in a difficult or slow market, you may consider giving your agent a 90-day authority. If the estate agent asks for an authority longer than 90 days, they are not confident that they can sell your property.

If you have not sold your property before the authority period expires, it does not mean that you have to sack the agent and start again. If you are satisfied with the agent's effort and service, you can still continue to work with them. However, if after 120–150 days you still have been unable to sell, regardless of how much you like your agent it is time for a fresh start and a new approach. As I explained earlier, once your property has been listed for this period, you are unlikely to achieve the price your property deserves.

Summary

- One of the benefits of investing in property is that your effort can make a difference.
- Improving the presentation of your property before sale is one of the best ways to involve yourself in increasing the value of your investment.
- Buyers will often consider a house where they liked the outside but not the inside. The converse is almost never true.
- When renovating, start at the front and work to-

wards the back fence. A property with an attractive exterior will always get more enquiries from potential buyers and tenants.

- When presenting an empty house, it must be spotlessly clean, as buyers will notice every imperfection. If presenting an occupied house, you may remove large pieces of furniture to make the rooms appear larger, but leave enough personal items on display to keep it looking lived-in.

- In the *kitchen*, cleanliness is of prime importance. Eliminate cooking odors and rubbish smells, while creating pleasant smells with candles, flowers, etc. Keep fridge magnets to a minimum (zero if possible). Clear benches and food preparation areas to make them look as large as possible.

- Adding candles, fluffy new towels, scented soaps, towel rails, and new mirrors will improve the appearance of the *bathroom*. Make sure beds are made in the *bedrooms*, and keep the *laundry and toilet* impeccably clean.

- Playing soft background music will improve viewers' perception of your property.

- Listing your property at the right price is crucial. Do your own research, employ an independent sworn valuer for a valuation, or list your property for sale without a price.

- Use a tiered commission structure, which gives a

bonus commission rate on amounts above a nominated sale price, to give the correct incentive for your real-estate agent to sell your property for the best possible price.

- Real estate is a numbers game. Your aim should be to get 50 or more potential buyers to inspect your property in the first 30 to 60 days after listing. Your advertising and marketing should have this as its aim. From these 50 plus inspections, you will normally have four or five buyers re-inspect. Buyers rarely purchase a property after only one inspection.

- If you are getting plenty of inspections but no re-inspections, you must immediately address any issues with presentation or price before your promotion loses its effect and the buyers stop coming.

- On average, you will get one offer for every 15 to 20 inspections through a property. From your 50 plus inspections you are likely to get three offers, one of which may be the winner.

- Home opens are the most convenient way to show multiple buyers through your property at the same time, and create a sense of urgency by making buyers feel as though they are in competition for your property.

- Any agent can sell your property for 95–100% of what it's worth. The best agents are those who will sell it for more.

- Test prospective agents' negotiation skills during your selection process by seeing if they will accept a lesser commission. An agent who fails to extract their desired commission with you will struggle to get the best price from buyers. Choose an agent with the ability and discipline to extract the maximum price buyers are willing to pay.
- Give your selected agents a maximum authority of 60 days to sell your property, or 90 days in a slow, difficult market.

4. Financial literacy

Before anyone panics, this chapter does not suggest that you get an accounting degree, or that you need to be fluent reading the financial reports published by BHP Billiton or any other major company. I do, however, suggest that you need to understand how to manage money.

This may seem simple enough. We make money and we spend it. We should not spend more than we make. But if it's so simple, *why do so many people struggle to pay their bills and balance their books each month?*

What is financial literacy?

At the start of this book I posed the question, "have you ever dreamt of winning Tattslotto?" Well, many thousands of people around the world have not only dreamt this—it has become their reality. For such instant millionaires, it would seem all their financial worries are behind them. Unfortunately, though, winning the lottery does not guarantee that you will be happy and wealthy. In many cases, the reality is just the opposite, and this demonstrates the importance of financial literacy.

A study of 35,000 major lottery winners in America, conducted by economists at the University of Kentucky, University of Pittsburgh, and Vanderbilt University found that within five years of their win, those lottery winners were twice as likely as members of the general population to file for bankruptcy.[5]

The researchers offered a few theories about why so many winners went bust. The primary reason given was that the winners tended to have limited financial literacy. This may not come as a great surprise, but I think most of us would assume that if we won a lottery, the same thing wouldn't happen to us. But it well could, if we are not financially literate, because lottery tickets are not a wealth creation plan.

We can put this another way: having money or assets at one point in time is only one of the two essential conditions for creating lasting wealth. The other is financial literacy.

So, what *is* financial literacy?

To be financially literate means having at least

[5]Scott Hankins, Mark Hoekstra, and Paige Marta Skiba, "The Ticket to Easy Street? The Financial Consequences of Winning the Lottery," *The Review of Economics and Statistics*, 93, no. 3 (August 2011), 961–969.

a sound basic knowledge of how to manage your money. You can balance your bills each month. You are capable of saving. You can make a budget and stick to it.

Financial literacy also means that you know what interest is and how it is charged, which debts should be paid off first, what negative gearing is, what an individual credit report is, and how to tell good debt from bad.

I have written in depth about some of these topics in *How to Buy Unlimited Investment Properties*, and to avoid repeating myself will only cover those items briefly here. Nevertheless, I believe managing money effectively is such an important life skill that I will recap all of the most important points.

I should also mention that there are many, many books that are entirely devoted to the topic of financial literacy. If you are having difficulty paying your bills each month, saving money, or setting and sticking to a budget, please find and read some of these books. Some of my personal favourites are from Robert Kiyosaki's *Rich Dad* series. His classic *Rich Dad, Poor Dad*, is a good starting point: it's easy to read and has a clear, practical approach that you can get out there and follow.

If you *can't* budget, pay your bills, and save, you won't only find it difficult to create wealth—you will find it difficult to live. You may have unconsciously created bad habits for yourself that you will need to change. If you do not make changes, things will stay the same and you will have to live with the consequences. If you have bad habits, you could pass these on to your children without realising or meaning to. For instance, if you can't save and live with constantly mounting debts, your children will consider this normal and may continue the same cycle in their adulthood.

Interest

We know that lending institutions charge us interest on borrowings. That's how they make money. We also understand the basic concept that the lower the interest rate they charge, the better it is for us.

When taking out a loan, in addition to the interest rate you also need to consider:

- what other fees the lender charges, such as establishment fees and monthly transaction fees
- what a comparison rate is and how it relates to the interest rate
- what penalties apply for late payments
- how often should you pay (weekly, fortnightly, or monthly for home or investment loans)

- whether you should fix the interest rate or keep it variable,
- if you should you pay "principal and interest" or "interest only" on your loan

I am not a financial planner, and you should not consider this section financial advice. If you feel you need such advice, please seek out the services of a qualified professional. The solution to many of the financial issues that you may face, particularly as a property investor, will depend on your personal circumstances and the economic climate at the time.

Nevertheless, you need to consider each item I have mentioned when you are thinking about borrowing money. Also be aware that knowing the answers to these questions is one thing: knowing how to act accordingly and apply it to your life is another.

I know people who I have considered very astute, and who even work in the financial industry, that have chosen to make extra payments off a low-interest home loan rather than a maxed-out, high-interest credit card. Sometimes we do things because they feel right, but when it comes to managing money we need to apply logic to make sure that we get the best outcome.

Because the economic climate is constantly changing, I cannot tell you which lending institution will have the best interest rate and other conditions tomorrow. But if you are aware that lending institutions make their money from charging you interest *and other fees*, you will be able to compare their offerings adequately, work out what a particular loan will really cost you, and choose the best option available to you at the time.

The comparison rate

To make it easier to compare products, Australian lenders are now obliged by law to show a *comparison rate* when advertising a loan interest rate. The comparison rate is included to help consumers calculate the true cost of a loan. It includes the interest rate and all fees and charges relating to that loan. When searching for a loan, most borrowers compare the different interest rates charged by lending institutions. But on its own, the interest rate does not take into account additional fees, such as establishment fees and ongoing costs.

A comparison rate is generated for a specific loan used as an example, and includes the following:

- the amount of the loan
- the term of the loan
- the repayment frequency
- the interest rate
- the fees associated with the loan

The loan amount and terms used to show the comparison rate will most likely differ from the exact loan you want to obtain. As a result, your particular loan may not be included in the comparison rate schedule, and you will have to calculate the comparison rate for your situation.

As an example, a recent advertisement in a major daily newspaper from one of the leading banks promoted a home loan with a variable rate of 4.8% and a comparison rate of 4.82%, based on a loan amount of $150,000 over 25 years. This comparison rate shows the true cost of this loan, but if you change any of the variables—e.g. if you increase the loan amount or lengthen or shorten the term of the loan—the comparison rate will also change. To cover this possibility, the same advertisement also carried a warning in small print at the bottom stating, "This comparison rate is only true for the example given. Different terms, fees or other loan amounts might result in a different comparison rate."

Principal-and-interest loans versus interest-only loans

Interest-only loans are becoming more popular with property investors because they let you minimise your mortgage repayments. Just as you'd expect, interest-only loans require the borrower to repay only the interest on the loan, as opposed to a standard principal-and-interest loan where you repay part of the loan amount along with the interest each time you make a payment.

As an example, if you buy an investment property and borrow $300,000 on an interest-only loan at 7%, your weekly repayments would be $404. However, if you borrowed the same amount using a principal-and-interest loan, your weekly payments would jump up to $534 per week.

I prefer interest-only loans for two reasons. The most important is that by using interest-only loans I can minimise my mortgage repayments. With the extra money I keep each week, I can afford to live and buy a few extra luxuries. The other reason I like interest-only loans is that regardless of how many sacrifices I make and how much money I pay off the loan's principal, the property does not grow in value any faster. In other words, paying off the mortgage is not related to capital growth.

I prefer to keep my repayments to a minimum as by doing this I can afford to buy more investment properties and continue servicing the debt. If I have excess funds and I want to use them to pay off a loan and further minimise my repayments and the interest charged, I can make a lump sum payment. If

I have this possibility in mind, I make sure that the loan has redraw facilities so I can retrieve this money if needed and use it for another purpose.

Loan repayment frequency

If you choose a principal-and-interest loan over an interest-only loan, you will need to consider the frequency with which you make repayments. This may seem like a relatively easy decision, and as a result you may give it little thought—but it can make a significant difference to the amount of interest you pay and the life of the loan.

You might choose to make monthly mortgage repayments because you get paid once a month and you can align your repayments with your paydays. But if you made fortnightly or weekly repayments, you would repay your loan faster and save on the interest charges.

Here's how it works.

If you make monthly repayments of $2,000 on your loan, over a year you will pay $24,000 in total. If you change the frequency of your payments to fortnightly and your repayments are $1,000 each time, over the year you will pay $26,000. This is because there are only 12 months in a year, but 26 fortnights. Because interest on a loan is usually calculated on a daily basis, by increasing your payments you can pay back the loan faster and reduce the amount of interest you pay.

As an example, Table 4 shows the saving you can make on a $330,000 loan, over the life of the loan, based on a 6.23% interest rate.

	Monthly	Fortnightly	Weekly
Repayments	$2,028	$1,014	$507
Total interest	$399,635	$306,731	$305,191
Interest saved	$0	$92,904	$94,444

Based on a 6.23% variable interest rate over 30 years.

Table 4: Comparison of loan-repayment frequencies

In this example, the monthly repayments on the loan would be $2,028 and the total interest you would pay over the 30-year life of the loan would be $399,635. By simply changing the frequency of your repayments from monthly to fortnightly, you would pay a total of $306,731 over the life of the loan, and as a result you would save almost $93,000.

Credit cards

It is probably fair to say that Australians have a love affair with credit cards. The situation is no different for most places in the developed world, including the US and the UK.

According to the Reserve Bank of Australia, there were 15.41 million credit cards in circulation in Australia in July 2013, with a total balance owing of $49.19 billion.[6] These figures continue to rise steadily.

Like many people, I have a credit card, and love the freedom and convenience it provides. But while there are many good reasons to have a credit card, such as offers of up to 45 days interest free on your purchases, loyalty reward points that in some cases can be redeemed as cash, and the obvious convenience it provides when you are not carrying cash, you must use a credit card responsibly.

If you own a credit card, you must pay the outstanding balance in full every month. If you do this, credit cards are wonderful. If you cannot manage this, then get rid of your card and pay for goods with cash or a debit card linked directly to your savings account.

You must be disciplined with credit cards. If you

---

[6]"Credit Card Statistics," accessed 6 February 2015, creditcard finder.com.au/credit-card-statistics.

are not, they will end up costing you a small fortune in interest charges and late fees. As a result, many Australians become buried in debt and struggle to get on top of credit card bills that grow steadily month after month because they could not meet their previous month's commitments. The interest rates charged on credit cards are incredibly high, and are only slightly better than the rate you would be charged by Bruno the Bruiser or whatever your local loan shark is called.

To educate us and make us aware of the costs involved, in Australia credit-card providers must now show on their monthly statements how long it would take to repay the balance and how much we would be charged in interest over that time if we only make the minimum monthly payment. These clearly show what the financial burden will be if you fail to pay your card in full each month, which is often decades of repayments and tens of thousands of dollars in interest.

Unfortunately, many people do not heed the warnings and continually use their cards to spend more than they can afford to repay at the end of the month. When their card has reached its limit, they increase it or get a new card to pay off the old card while continuing to rack up debts. Credit cards are the easiest type of loan to get, but they are undoubtedly the worst way to borrow due to the high interest and associated fees. Almost anyone with a regular income can get a credit card, but unfortunately not everyone is disciplined enough to use one correctly.

If governments and lending institutions were genuinely concerned about helping people manage their credit card debts better, they would make consumers pay at least 50% of their credit-card debt each month, would not allow consumers to increase their credit card limit until the current outstanding amount has been paid in full, and would not allow people to get new or additional cards until their current card balance was zero.

Obviously lending institutions do not concur with my view, because they invite consumers who are already struggling to pay their current bills to increase their limit. If you are struggling financially, more credit may seem very attractive, but all it does is help the debt spiral out of control.

Finally, you need to be aware of the impact a credit card has on your borrowing capacity. If you have a credit card and want to apply for a home loan, the financial institution will assume that your credit card is at its limit regardless of what the current balance is. In other words, if you have a card with a $10,000 limit, the bank will assume that you owe

$10,000 and have to make repayments based on that level of liability. Even if you show that on average you only spend $2,000 each month on your card, the lender will only take the credit card limit into consideration. This is because you could make those extra borrowings at any time.

This can significantly affect your borrowing capacity. Every $5,000 of credit available on your card equates to $15,000 less that you can borrow on a home loan. The reason is simple: the interest charged on your credit card is about three times higher than the interest charged on your home loan. If you want to borrow more money for a home, reduce your credit card limit. Better still, get rid of your credit card altogether.

The two most important rules to remember are:

1. Pay off your credit card in full every month
2. If you cannot pay off your credit-card debt each month, look at consolidating it into another loan with a lower interest rate

If you need help doing this, I urge you to get independent financial advice. Only if you have mastered debt can you financially prosper.

Good debt versus bad debt

Growing up, I was taught that all debt is bad and should be avoided wherever possible. It was with this in mind that I resisted getting a credit card until a girlfriend pointed out to me all the things I could buy her if I had a little plastic card in my wallet. After that lesson, my life was never the same.

My life also changed when I bought my first home, as it does for many young people. For many, getting your first mortgage—which comes with the responsibility to make weekly, fortnightly, or monthly payments—it is akin to reaching adulthood. Time and again, older people emphasised how important it was to make these payments on time, and to pay as much as I could above the minimum requirement to reduce the loan period and the amount of interest I would pay.

As regular as a Swiss timepiece, I obediently made my payments and scrimped so I could contribute more than the minimum requirement. As I had learnt that all debt was bad, I worked as hard as I could to pay it off as quickly as possible.

Now that my hair is greyer and a little sparser, I have decided that not only is some debt good—it is essential if you are going to create untold riches. Clearly, this is a philosophical shift from what I was taught, but I learned it through experience and these kinds of lessons are the best of all.

I now believe debt is necessary to truly create wealth. This is because debt allows you to control a large asset base. If the asset grows in value, you can become very, very wealthy. As we know, real estate is an asset class with a proven track record of growth. But not all debt is good—just as not all debt is bad. The crucial difference is who pays off the debt: you, or someone else.

Bad debt

If you pay the debt, meaning that you make all the repayments from your personal savings or income, and if there are no tax concessions, *this is bad debt.*

You must limit this kind of debt. If uncontrolled, it can grow to the point where you run out of money to make the repayments and you will go bankrupt.

Good debt

This type of debt can still be in your name, or the name of your company or trust name, and it is still ultimately your responsibility to repay it. Good debt, however, has the advantage that someone else helps you pay it and tax concessions can apply.

Borrowings to buy rental property are a common example of this kind of debt. When you buy an investment property, you organise a loan from the bank in your name (or your company/trust's name). Naturally, you need to repay this loan—but instead of just relying on your income, you also receive rental income from the tenant. If you buy the right investment property, the rental income can be sufficient to cover the loan repayments in their entirety. In this case, the investment property is positively geared.

If the rental income is insufficient to cover the repayments, you will need to contribute your own money to help make them. This is known as negative gearing. If this applies, you can claim tax deductions.

As I have mentioned, I now believe you must embrace good debt to truly become wealthy, because it lets you control larger assets. Coming to realise this represented a fundamental shift in my thinking.

What changed my mind was that after purchasing my first investment property, I wanted to buy more. But with the loan on that first investment property, I wanted to pay off that loan as quickly as possible, just as I had paid off all the loans I had before. I had a principal-and-interest loan on that property, and made extra payments whenever possible. Eventually, I saw that by increasing my repayments, the principal-and-interest loan reduced my ability to borrow and fulfil my goal of building my portfolio.

Now I take out interest-only loans, and do not

worry about paying off the principal. I know that my portfolio looks after itself. The rental income services the debt and the asset continues to grow in value.

I had to learn to become comfortable with debt. Buying more than one investment property meant borrowing more money, and it didn't take long for my debt levels to soar. Depending on your attitude this debt can be alarming—but it could also be exciting, because it represents an opportunity to increase your wealth.

Over time, I became increasingly comfortable with debt, as I needed to. The time it could take for others to do the same will vary. My wife, who was raised with similar values and attitudes toward money as I was, has a lower tolerance for debt. If you are in a partnership like this, it is important that you recognise others may have different attitudes to debt, and that you set clear goals and targets you all agree with. That way, everyone has input and takes ownership of what you want to achieve.

Each time you purchase a new investment property, you increase your level of good debt. After you have determined how your investment is geared and the rental income and loan repayments become something you take for granted, you will become tolerant to this kind of debt and confident in taking on more. You will also understand more clearly how good debt and bad debt are different. Then the key question will be how much good debt you want to take on.

Your credit report

If you have ever applied for credit, a phone account, store card, or hire-purchase agreement, you will have a credit report. A credit report can be assessed by lenders, including banks, credit unions, and utility companies, to track your credit history. These reports are used to determine your ability to service a new loan or credit card, or any limit increase on existing cards or loans.

If you want to borrow to invest, achieving and maintaining a good credit report is vital.

It is a good idea to regularly check your credit report to make sure that there are no errors that could adversely affect your ability to get credit. You can order a free copy of your report from credit reporting agencies every year, provided you can wait 10 days to receive it. You can also pay a fee to the agency to receive it quicker, or to have them monitor your individual report and notify you whenever a change is made.

Your individual credit report will include the following information.

Personal details	Your name, date of birth, current and past postal address, employment detail and driver's licence number.
Joint applicant	A joint applicant's name will appear if you have previously applied for credit with another person
Credit cards	Information about any credit cards you hold.
Arrears brought up to date	Any debts that were unpaid or overdue and have now been paid or settled.
Defaults	Defaults or any other credit infringements that are 60 days or more overdue and where debt collection activity has started.
Credit applications	Any credit you have applied for.
Debt agreements	Any court orders, bankruptcy, debt agreements, or personal insolvency agreements in your name.

Table 5: Your individual credit report

New information in your credit report

Repayment History

If you are in Australia, information about your repayment history on credit accounts, like your home loan, personal loans, and credit cards, has been collected from December 2012. Beginning in March 2014, under new laws lenders can access a much bigger dossier about an individual's credit habits and focus not just on negative information including defaults, bankruptcies, and court judgments, but also on positive information about an applicant such as their ability to pay back a loan.

Repayment history information will include:

- whether or not you have made payments by the due date (zero payment or partial payment by the due date will be considered as missed payments)
- the dates on which you made any payments that had been in arrears (but not the amounts you missed)

Your credit report will not include information about your repayment history for the following types of bills:

- utilities (gas, water, and electricity)

- phone bills (mobiles, home phone, and internet)

From March 2014, your credit report will also list any commercial or business loans you have applied for, and it will list any credit providers who have requested a copy of your credit report.

Defaults on your credit report

If you fail to make a payment on a debt, your credit provider can refer that debt to a debt collector, report it to a credit reporting agency, and request that the agency record the default on your credit report.

A credit provider can only report your debt if:

- The default amount is $150 or more.
- You are a confirmed missing debtor or clearout, which means that your creditor cannot contact you.
- 60 days or more have passed since the due date for payment.
- The creditor has asked you to pay the debt either in person or in writing.

The credit provider must advise you that they may lodge a report about the overdue payment before they do so. Usually, your credit contract or service agreement will explain when your credit provider may make a report about you to a credit reporting agency.

How long will a default be listed?

A default listing remains on your credit report for five years, or seven years in the case of a clear-out. If you pay the debt, the listing still remains on your report but will be update to reflect that you have made payments.

When you apply for credit later, you could be rejected if there is a default listed on your credit report.

As I have mentioned, it is essential that you maintain a good credit report—which means it is crucial that you *check* your credit report. A credit reporting agency or credit provider may have reported information incorrectly or inaccurately, and this could have a disastrous effect on your ability to obtain credit. Typically, borrowers become aware of their credit report when they have a credit application declined. We might not even be aware that credit reports exist until our own creates an issue for us.

If there are any mistakes in your report, you can have them changed or removed.

On one occasion, I ordered a copy of my credit report and discovered an entry related to a deposit bond supposedly for $2.85 million—in fact the amount had only been $180,000. I raised this with the credit provider and credit reporting agency, and had the mistake corrected. Had I not discovered this error, I most likely would not have been able to secure my next loan, which would have prevented me from settling investment properties I had bought.

Managing your credit report is an easy way of saving a significant amount of time and trouble the next time you apply for credit. By checking your report regularly, you can ensure that lenders are getting a balanced, informed picture of your financial health.

Your balance sheet

Many people will think that a balance sheet is something used exclusively by businesses. Well, it's true that all businesses use balance sheets, but balance sheets are not the exclusive domain of businesses. In fact, you can use balance sheets for all sorts of things. Everyone has most likely used a very simple version of a balance sheet to make a list of pros and cons. A balance sheet is just like a list of pros and cons, but the left column lists all your assets and the right column lists all your liabilities.

All businesses have a balance sheet, and I want you to think of your investment portfolio as a business where you are the CEO. Every good CEO knows exactly what is in their business's balance sheet, and more particularly what the bottom line looks like.

Of course, we would like to have more assets in the left column than liabilities in the right. You can easily achieve this by including in your asset list personal items such as furniture, car(s), and superannuation. These items will not be taken into consideration if you are applying for a loan, but as I explained in *How to Buy Unlimited Investment Properties*, if you show these items and your loan application is hanging in the balance, the final decision will often be left to the lending manager's discretion. By showing these items it appears that you have not been a sieve when it comes to money, and that you have some assets to show for the income you have made. This is particularly important if you have little or no savings in your bank account.

By having a balance sheet, you can start to appreciate how a lending manager will view your personal financial position. Does it look healthy? Are there too many items listed in the liability column? Do you need to start consolidating some debt? What does the bottom line look like?

Just like the CEO of a business, you need to be

aware of every item in your balance sheet. When you start to analyse it and break all the information down to just numbers, it will remove any of the emotional or sentimental attachments you may have toward some of your assets. You will see the items in the assets column for what they are: assets you have acquired to build your wealth and financial freedom. You will truly start to think about which of those assets you would like to hold onto forever, and what assets are dispensable. You will also start to critically look at the liability column and begin thinking strategically about how you can best reduce this column or, better yet, how you can get rid of the debt altogether. The process of analysing your balance sheet can be very empowering, helping you open your mind and identify creative ways to effectively manage your portfolio of assets and plan for the future.

You will need to provide your bank or lending institution with the information on your balance sheet every time you apply for a new loan or refinance an existing one, so it pays to keep the information up to date. Whenever you revalue a property, update your balance sheet. If you dispose of an asset or buy a new one … update your balance sheet.

Once you have made a balance sheet, I recommend adding a few columns for your own personal information. In one column, show your monthly repayment amount for any loans in the liabilities column. In the next column, show the loan interest rate. In the column after, include information about the type of loan—variable, fixed, or combination. If the loan is fixed, also list when the fixed term expires.

In the next column, I list the rental income that corresponds to the investment properties in the assets column. If you show the rental income as a weekly, fortnightly, or monthly figure, make sure that you also show the loan repayments for the same interval. That way you can easily compare the figures to see if your investment is costing you money or making it.

In the next column, list when the rental leases will expire. In the column after, show the expiration dates of landlord insurance policies and, if applicable, the building insurance policy you have for each investment property. Finally, in the last column list the date that you purchased each investment property and, if applicable, the date you last had it last refinanced or valued.

All this information is particularly useful when you sell an investment property and you need to go back to old tax returns and find information relating to its purchase price and acquisition costs.

I include these extra columns because they make

my balance sheet a convenient single reference point for information about my investment properties. Having this information at my fingertips, I am less likely to let an insurance policy expire or a lease end without discussing it with the managing real-estate agent. As your portfolio grows, it will become more difficult to remember exactly when you bought a property or when you last had a property valued. A simple chart can save you a lot of work later on, and it could save you from a situation where you don't receive an insurance policy renewal notice in the mail and so let a policy expire right before you find yourself needing to claim on it.

With all these extra columns added, your comprehensive balance sheet will look something like the one in Tables 6 and 7. Note that the extra columns make the table too wide to print easily: you will want to use Excel or a similar spreadsheet program to manage and view your information.

Cash flow

Now that you have your balance sheet, you know your exact financial position and what you are worth. Now you need to make sure that you can afford your lifestyle.

Asset	Purchase price	Liabilities	Repayments /month	%	Loan terms	Rent /month	...
1 Invest. St	$400K	$350K	$2.1K	6.00%	Variable	$2.3K	...
2 Invest. St	$350K	$300K	$2K	6.30%	Variable	$1.9K	...
3 Invest. St	$450K	$450K	$2.5K	5.95%	F 4 Dec. 2015	$2.45K	...
Car	$25K						...
Furnishings	$20K						...
Super.	$60K						...
Total	$1.35m	$1.1m	$6.6K			$6.65K	...

F = fixed

Table 6: Your comprehensive balance sheet (Part 1)

Asset			Lease expiry	Insurance expiry	Purchase date
1 Invest. St	…		9 Feb. 2015	L 13 Sep. 2014	10 Feb. 2012
2 Invest. St	…		12 Mar. 2015	L 1 Jul 2014	R 3 Mar. 2013
				B 3 Aug 2014	15 Sep. 2010
3 Invest. St	…		Periodic	L 29 Oct. 2014	11 Sep. 2014

B = building insurance   R = refinance date   L = landlord insurance

Table 7: Your comprehensive balance sheet (Part 2)

I don't subscribe to the philosophy that says you should spend the money you need to live the lifestyle you want and in the end you will find some way to afford it. As we know, credit is everywhere and it is readily available to individuals, businesses, and even countries. The problem with credit is that it eventually has to be paid back. Credit can give you a billionaire's lifestyle for a short period of time, but ultimately it has to be paid for or you will end up buried in debt. If you reach that point, it can be a very long way back to being debt-free.

A far more prudent way for individuals, businesses, and governments to operate is to spend within their means and limit their use of credit to the absolute minimum. In other words: *only spend what you have, to buy things you can afford.*

The number one priority for any responsible business is to stay solvent, and the lifeblood of every business is cash flow. If a business is not solvent but continues to trade and in so doing incurs more expenses it cannot repay, the directors could be held personally liable and may even go to jail. As a result, a good business pays all its bills when due and holds onto enough working capital to keep running .

You should apply this same philosophy to your personal banking habits and your investment portfolio. You must remain solvent!

Following this rule will already be second nature to the many readers who balance their household books every month. These people have no difficulty managing money; they can even manage to save money. For others, finding enough money each month is a constant struggle and saving is nothing but a fantasy.

If you belong to the group that struggles each month, how do you make sure you remain solvent?

First, compare your expenses with your income. Most people know what their personal income is, and if they have a spouse or partner, what their household income is. That's the easy part. Many people find it more difficult to determine what their expenses are.

All expenses can be categorised into two sections: *essential* and *non-essential* expenses.

Essential expenses can't be avoided and are essential for living. Many of these are fixed, which makes them easy to identify and budget for. They include:

- rent or mortgage repayments
- insurances
- electricity
- school fees
- car services
- healthcare
- rates
- food
- water
- clothing
- petrol

Non-essential expenses could be avoided. They

are not mandatory, but optional, or discretionary. You can choose to avoid them. Many non-essential items are luxuries: you don't need them to live. They include:

- entertainment
- clothing
- gambling
- vacations
- pets
- petrol

Some items appear on both the essential and non-essential lists. The line between essential and non-essential can be blurry. Clothing, for instance, is something we must have. But you can shop at Target or at Harrods—it's your choice. You can buy a business suit for $200, or a similar one for $1,000. One suit is essential, two suits are preferable, three suits are nice, but the line between essential and non-essential becomes more blurred with each new suit you acquire. Do you need five suits or 20? Shopping is now a leisure activity for many people, a socially accepted pastime and a normal weekend outing. But usually, when we shop we spend. We may tell ourselves that buying a particular item is essential because we need it, but in reality our lives are no worse for not having it.

Likewise, petrol appears on both lists. Running your car to get to work to make money or drop your kids off at school is essential, but it is not essential to drive interstate for a holiday. As we know, petrol is expensive. Some trips are a necessary part of life, but others are for pleasure.

We don't list essential and non-essential expenses with the aim of stopping doing what we enjoy in life. Rather, we want to make ourselves aware that some things are vital to our sustenance, while others decorate our lives and make them more interesting—but remain optional.

When you have made your list of essential items, you can allocate a cost to each of them. I suggest you make this a yearly figure and compare it to your net (after-tax) annual salary or household income. My hope is that the essential items will add up to significantly less than your income. The amount left is yours to spend on those items on your non-essential list.

A word of warning, though. I would add an extra 10% to the total cost of your essentials and call it "miscellaneous". This will hopefully be enough to cover unexpected costs that could pop up through the year, as well as price increases to the items you have listed.

When you have calculated the amount you have left to spend on non-essential items, divide it by twelve so you know what you can spend each month. If you overspend in one month, you must make up for it by spending less in the following month to bring your expenses back into balance. If one month you spend less than your allowance, you can save the money or spend a little bit extra the next month.

The vital thing is that you live within your means. Any person, business, or country that fails to do this will eventually become insolvent and go broke.

Because it is so essential to live within your means, look closely at your cash flow before buying another investment property. After buying an investment property, it takes me about six months to become accustomed to the extra activity in my bank account. Once that period has passed, I can accurately gauge how my cash flow is going.

Usually, after buying an investment property there are extraordinary (one-off) expenses you will incur in the short term. These may include new light fittings, window furnishings, carpets, and painting. Once these have been paid for, you will also have the real-estate agent's letting fees and marketing fees.

Usually, after six months an investment property's income and expenses get into a regular routine, and it becomes an established and standard pattern of movement in the owner's cash flow.

Of course, everyone is different; some readers will buy investment properties quicker than others. It does not matter how quickly or slowly you grow your investment portfolio, as long as you remain solvent and pay *all* your expenses, essential and non-essential alike.

Avoid late fees

My final recommendation in this chapter is pay all your bills on time, particularly your loan repayments. If you don't, late fees can apply. These are usually a set amount regardless of how late the repayment is. In other words, the same fee applies if you are one day late or a week late. That doesn't mean if you are late making a repayment you can take your time catching up, because in addition to the late fee penalty interest rates also apply, making your debt grow faster. What it *does* mean is that paying on time or early is essential: if you are even one day late, it will cost you.

To help avoid late fees on your investment property loan, I strongly recommend you always keep enough money in your bank account to cover another month's repayment. If your monthly repayment is $2,000, make sure you always have that much cash in your account on top of any rent you would normally receive.

The reason I suggest this is because if you rely on

just your rental income each month to meet your loan repayments, one day you will miss a repayment and be charged late fees. I have seen this countless times: the tenant may have missed or been late paying rent one month, the estate agency may have been closed over a holiday period, or extraordinary expenses may have been incurred during the month. Unfortunately, from time to time things occur that are beyond our control. On those occasions, you can find yourself without money in your bank account.

Typically, when this occurs, the landlord contacts their estate agency and complains bitterly that they have incurred a late fee because they missed a repayment. Most often, the late fee is charged for missing a repayment by only one day. As soon as they become aware of the problem, the landlord transfers money into the investment loan account from elsewhere. But by then it is too late: they have already incurred the late fee.

This is why I so strongly recommend that you always have enough money in your investment loan account to cover at least one month's repayment. If you don't, at some point you will miss a repayment and incur a late fee. I can practically guarantee it. By keeping that extra money in your account, you have the comfort of knowing you will never miss a payment. When the inevitable happens and the rent is late or not paid one month, you can relax and take your time investigating the cause without worrying about the effect.

Summary

- Having a significant amount of money at one point in time is just one of the conditions of building real wealth: the other is financial literacy.
- Financial literacy means having a good basic knowledge of how to manage your money: how to save, develop a budget and sticking to it, knowing where to invest, and understanding credit reports, debt, and interest.
- When taking out a property investment loan, be sure to consider not just the interest rate, but also the comparison rate, penalties, the frequency of payments, whether the rate is fixed or variable, and whether you will repay principal and interest or interest only.
- Credit-card holders should pay their balance in full every month or consider consolidating it into another loan with a lower interest rate
- Know the difference between good and bad debt. You take on *bad debt* when you borrow to pay for consumer goods or unprofitable investments, and

the repayments come solely from your personal savings or income. You take on *good debt* when you borrow to buy an asset that delivers an income or return, possibly with related tax concessions, and that return (i.e. rent) makes or helps you make the repayments on your debt.

- Good debt that lets you control a large asset base is extremely helpful for creating wealth.
- Know how to obtain and understand your personal credit report, which will be assessed by lenders when you want to take out or refinance a loan. This could save you a significant amount of time and trouble when getting credit.
- Know how to create and manage your personal balance sheet, which lists all your assets and liabilities, and is an essential starting point for managing your assets and planning for the future.
- Cash flow is the lifeblood of every business. To manage your own cash flow, only spend what you have, to buy things you can afford. Minimise non-essential expenses, and economise on essential expenses, to maximise the amount you have to invest as you work towards financial freedom.

5. *The best time to sell*

Selling real estate is just like selling any other product: the most important influences on the price you get are supply and demand. When there are more buyers than sellers, prices go up; when there are more sellers, prices fall.

Even though price movements in real estate have such a simple cause behind them, many myths persist about sales.

The most widely known of these is that spring is the best time to sell. It gains further traction every year, because estate agents reiterate it every spring in an attempt to attract more listings. It also persists because like many myths, it contains a significant element of truth.

In spring the sun shines, birds sing, flowers bloom, and more people look through estate agents' home opens. Auction crowds are larger, and agents sell more properties than in any other season. On the surface, it appears that spring is indeed the best time to sell. But the immediate perception that properties sell easily in spring does not take into consideration some other vital statistics, particularly *clearance rates*

163

and *time on the market.*

Estate agents' main argument as to why spring is the best time to sell is, "we sell more homes in spring than any other time." This is true— because they list more homes for sale in spring than at any other time of year.

During winter, real estate largely goes into hibernation. Winter is cold and bleak, and far fewer homes are listed for sale. As a result, sales drop off. After winter, spring is a period of excitement, anticipation, and expectation. Estate agents throw off their jackets and enthusiastically list every property they possibly can during spring. They understand that their competitors are doing exactly the same thing, and that to maintain and grow their market share they need to list all properties that come their way—big and small, cheap and expensive alike. They will list anything they can get their hands on. If they control the listings, they will make money.

Sales volumes naturally increase because of all these new properties being listed. Properties are sold and commissions are made. Seemingly, everyone is jubilant, and the cycle continues year after year. But following the herd and listing your property at the same time as everyone else is not necessarily the best strategy if you want to sell for the best possible price.

Supply and demand

To explain why following the herd isn't the best strategy, we need to take a good look at how supply and demand work when selling your property.

Demand

Demand for a new property comes from people wanting to buy a home for the first time, families expanding and shrinking, job transfers, marriage and divorce, and investors looking for their next buy. These reasons aren't seasonal. Like births, deaths, and marriages, they all occur throughout the year. As a result, *demand for real estate is a consistent straight line throughout the year.*

It is true that in spring, more people attend auctions and look through estate agents' home opens. This is because in spring, people venture out of their homes and explore their neighbourhoods. When they see an agent's board promoting an open home, they'll drop in and let the agent know how great the neighbours are. Likewise, people riding past on their bikes or taking the dog for a walk will also inspect a home for curiosity's sake.

These people are affectionately known as "tyre kickers." There is nothing wrong with tyre kickers, and in fact they serve a worthwhile function. They can help draw a crowd. After all, the best way to attract a crowd is to have one already. In spring, tyre kickers are as thick as new blooms in flower, but in winter they generally don't leave the comfort and warmth of their homes.

The seasons don't have the same impact on genuine buyers. These buyers have made it their mission to find and purchase the perfect property, to change their life for the better. Neither rain, hail, nor snow will dampen their enthusiasm. They will attend open homes and bid at auction whatever the weather. Their numbers don't fluctuate wildly like those of the tyre kickers. Real buyers are resilient, and are in the market the whole year through.

Supply

Unlike demand, supply varies enormously throughout the year. It's definitely seasonal, and has massive peaks and troughs.

When I was selling real estate in Melbourne, the estate agency I worked for would regularly list 100 or more new properties for auction every December. By contrast, in the quieter months, each year we would list far less: perhaps a dozen auctions in February and about 20 in June.

Of the 100-plus auctions we conducted every December, we would sell about 50%. But of the properties we auctioned in February and June, we would usually sell 100%. This figure, the proportion of properties that sell, is called the *clearance rate*, and as you can see, it can vary massively throughout the year.

In absolute numbers, it remains true that more properties are sold in December than June, because 50 out of 100 properties is still far more than 12 out of 12. But as a general rule, the more auctions that were held the lower the clearance rate would be. We recorded similar results year after year.

Of course, not all sellers list their property for auction. If you decide to use the traditional "for sale" method, variations in demand and supply will manifest in different ways. Here the key metric is *days on the market*. The more homes listed for sale in any period, the longer it will take for them to sell, on average. Of course, in any market, at any time, there will always be some properties that sell very quickly. But when you look at averages, you can see a very clear correlation between the time required to sell a property and the number of properties for sale at that time.

The graph in Figure 2 shows the typical number of auctions and the corresponding clearance rate over a 12-month period when I was working in Mel-

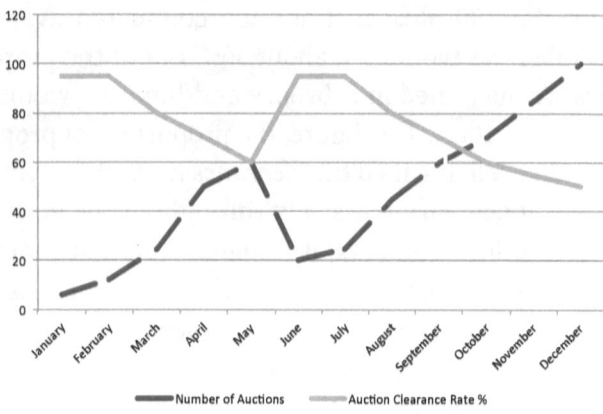

120
100
80
60
40
20
0

January February March April May June July August September October November December

Number of Auctions   Auction Clearance Rate %

Figure 2: Auction frequency and clearance throughout the year

bourne. As I mentioned, these results were typical, and when you consider the impact of demand versus supply, trends become apparent.

Of course, if you are a buyer, there is no better time to be looking than in spring. You will be spoilt for choice, as there's an incredible amount of properties to choose from. As an estate agent, it can be extremely challenging to negotiate with buyers during this period, because they will regularly point out that if their offer is declined they can take their money and buy the property recently listed for sale down the road.

Because of the large supply of properties on the market in spring, auction clearance rates drop, properties take longer to sell, prices are not as strong, and buyers' confidence grows—sometimes to the level of arrogance. Buyers often become more belligerent in their negotiations, because with each new property listed, they see more room to negotiate a larger price reduction.

Spring is definitely a buyer's market, and estate agents and buyers know it. Sellers could be discovering this for the first time. Because every spring is the same in this regard, whenever I sell one of my own properties, I pick a quieter time of year. Some people will say that I have missed the peak selling period, and they are right, but there are good opportunities either side of it.

Generally, I have favoured the warmer summer months to sell. The weather is still favourable for prospective buyers looking at properties, but there is far less for sale, and consequently, buyers have less choice. The number of properties for sale will increase again during the autumn months, but not to the levels of spring. As I mentioned, the real-estate market will slumber during winter. Personally, I have found that summer is a great time to sell, as you can see from the strong auction clearance rates and shorter average time spent on the market.

As with most rules in life, there are always exceptions to the observation that demand is constant throughout the year. For instance, if you have a property in a coastal area mainly made up of holiday homes, it may be appropriate to list your property when potential buyers are there, regardless of the season or how much competition. The buyers simply may not be there during the off season.

Likewise, if your property has a pool or a fantastic outdoor entertaining area and this is a key selling feature of your property, it could be beneficial to sell in summer even though there may be plenty of other homes for sale with a pool. The weather will make your unique selling point more attractive than it would be in winter. In a case like this, you need to present your property better than the competition and use superior pricing and marketing strategies.

Exceptional circumstances or events can also have an effect on auction clearance rates and time spent on the market. For instance, state and federal elections, an impending federal budget or a Reserve Bank interest rate announcement can reduce buyer confidence, skewing sales figures. But except for these isolated occasions, the general rule remains that to sell your property quicker and for a higher price, you are better off listing it when there are fewer properties to compete against.

Summary

- Supply and demand are the most important influences on real-estate prices.
- Supply varies enormously throughout the year, because many sellers choose to list in the peak selling periods—but this is when there are more homes competing for a buyer.
- Demand, on the other hand, stays consistent throughout the year, because the changing seasons don't have a strong effect on resilient buyers. "Tyre kickers" stay home when the weather turns cold and wet, but genuine buyers are in the market year-round.
- The more homes listed for sale at a particular time, the longer it will take for them to sell, on average.
- Summer is the best time to sell. There aren't as many properties on the market as in spring, but weather is still favourable for inspections. There are strong auction clearance rates and the average time on market is relatively short.

6. Rental return
or capital growth?

One of investors' most commonly asked questions is, "Should I look for an investment property that offers a high rental return, or one that will attract high capital growth?"

In a perfect world, you would find one property that offered both, which had a great rental return that made it neutrally or positively geared, and which attracted fantastic capital growth. These properties exist: to find them you just need to look carefully through the myriad of properties available. When looking for an investment property, the general rule is that the cheaper the property, the better the rental return will be, but the poorer its capital growth. The converse is also true: properties that are more expensive have a lower rental return but higher expected capital growth.

To put this in one statement, *there is generally an inverse relationship between rental yield and capital gains.*

So, which should you choose? Yield or capital gains? Each investor has their own thoughts and strategies, and each side can debate the merits of their case. There will never be a clear winner or a best answer.

The game of Monopoly is a great analogy for this complex question. Think about how you play. Do you buy the most expensive properties, like Mayfair, which attract the highest rents but require the most investment, or do you buy the cheaper properties like Old Kent Road, which appear to give a quicker and cheaper opportunity to collect rent? The same tactics apply to your investment portfolio: do you want a lot of cheaper properties, or are you happy with fewer, more expensive properties? Do you covet quantity over quality?

These questions keep the coffers filled for many financial planners and accountants. Clients seek advice to these seemingly irresolvable questions from these professionals—who may have no greater wisdom or insight than a 10-year-old child playing Monopoly.

Estate agents bless the financial planners and accountants who send their clients to them with instructions to buy a negatively geared investment property to lower their income tax bill. Agents love these novice investors because they are uneducated, have no real idea of what they should be looking for, and are easy to please. Any property can be turned into a negatively geared investment—you just lower the rent.

Build a balanced portfolio

So, what should you be looking for? As I mentioned, I do not believe there is a clear winner in this debate, but I would argue that your investment portfolio should include both types of property: those that offer a great rental return and those that will spectacularly increase in value in the future.

The key is to acquire an investment portfolio that is as close as possible to being neutrally geared. If you can do this, you will keep your options open in the future. If a fantastic investment opportunity presents itself, you will be able to afford it. If your investment portfolio is negatively geared, which means you are contributing your own money to pay the bills, when opportunity knocks you had better not be home. If every new investment takes more money out of your pocket each month, you will quickly reach the limit of your resources and will not be able to buy any more properties.

The reason for recommending an investment portfolio with both types of property is that positively geared properties with great rental returns will help pay for any negatively geared properties. This will balance your portfolio overall and keep the gearing neutral. If you just have lots of positively geared investment properties, your portfolio may not significantly grow in value. It will most likely underperform in capital growth and will not make you a lot of money in the future.

On the other hand, if you just have negatively geared properties, they could send you broke. Regardless of how big your income is, if you have to continuously contribute money to help pay the bills from your portfolio, there is a finite number of properties you can support before you run out of money—and we want the ability to buy *unlimited* investment properties if it suits us.

Some properties have high rental returns because historically they have not had significant capital growth. Rent increases have outpaced property price increases, making the property positively geared. Such properties, with weak histories of capital growth and equally weak expectations, have to be sold on the strength of their high rental returns. When these properties are listed for sale, they are advertised as being "a great investment" with a "strong rental history", "good tenant", and "fantastic return", representing a "wonderful opportunity."

Other properties have low rental returns because historically they have had significant capital growth. Rent increases have not kept pace with property prices, and the property has become negatively geared. Having grown in value significantly in the past, they also have a higher expectation of significant capital growth in the future. When these properties are listed for sale, they are not advertised as being great investments and the listings do not mention rental income. Marketing for these properties is aimed at owner occupiers, because with such low rental returns, very few investors can afford to buy them.

If you have a balanced, neutrally geared portfolio with both negatively and positively geared investment properties, you will be able to afford to hold onto your investments, and the portfolio as a whole will attract excellent capital growth and make you money.

Where to start?

If you are just starting on your journey of acquiring investment properties, I suggest you start with a positively geared property that offers a high rental return.

If you start with a positively geared property,

your first experience as a landlord will be a positive one. The investment will pay for itself and not be a financial burden, and you will buy another investment property. If you start with a negatively geared property, my concern for you is that you have purchased a financial burden and may not ever buy another investment property.

Although some financial planners and accountants will advise their clients to buy a negatively geared investment property, what harm can come from buying a positively geared property instead? You will make more money and as a result you will pay more tax. If you make money, you pay tax. If you make *more* money, you pay *more* tax. If this keeps you awake at night, stop working, or better still, donate money to charities. Although it may seem counterintuitive, *paying more tax is often a good thing—because it means you made more money.*

If you really want a negatively geared property so that you earn less and pay less tax, you can lower the rent on your investment property. This may not excite the taxman, but at least your financial planner and your tenant will be happy.

Summary

- Generally there is an inverse relationship between rental yield and capital growth. The better the rental return from your property, the less your expectation of capital gain should be, and vice versa.

- Cheaper properties generally have higher rental yields but lower capital growth, while more expensive properties have lower yields but better growth.

- Your property portfolio should include both kinds of property: high-yield/low-gain and low-yield/high-gain.

- Aim to create a portfolio that is *neutrally geared*, where positively geared high-yield/low-gain properties balance negatively geared, low-yield/high-gain properties.

- When building your portfolio, start with a positively geared high-yield property, which will put money in your pocket and increase your confidence and motivation to continue.

7. Use a property manager

In *How to Buy Unlimited Investment Properties*, I wrote about the importance of insurance. Having a qualified property manager look after your investment property is much like having a comprehensive insurance policy. If anything goes wrong with your investment property, the property manager, with the backing of his or her real-estate agency, is there to look after your important asset.

Correctly managing the lease on a rental property is an incredibly complicated and at times very difficult job. A good property manager needs to have great communication skills, so they can act as a mediator and often interpreter between the landlord and tenant. They also need to have exhaustive knowledge of legislation, incredible organisation, superb time-management skills, and the patience and calm of a Tibetan monk.

If you possess of all of these attributes yourself, you could consider managing your own investment property, but for reasons I will explain, I still don't recommend it.

Obviously, a property manager needs to wear lots

of different hats and possess many skills. It is a complex and specialised area of expertise, as you will see when I explain some of the roles a property manager must play.

Determining market rent

In *How to Buy Unlimited Investment Properties*, I covered how to carry out market research as part of your due diligence when you are buying a property or obtaining a new independent valuation. In the same way you carry out this research by looking for evidence of past sales, you can also research rents. Based on the evidence you collect, you can determine what is the fair market rent for your investment property.

The best way to determine what the rent should be is to find properties similar to yours that are currently being rented near your property. When comparing your property with others, some of the features you need to consider are:

- no. of bedrooms
- no. of bathrooms
- age of the property
- size of the property
- number of living areas
- heating
- air conditioning

- dishwasher
- garages
- sheds

Through their own database, and the databases they subscribe to, property managers have access to information about comparable rental properties located near yours, and can make the process of determining the appropriate rent much easier.

Rent reviews

Regular rent reviews are essential to ensure that you get the rent you deserve and achieve the maximum return on your investment. A property manager has a vast knowledge of what properties are renting for in the area. They also keep a computer system that automatically alerts them to review your rent.

Property managers perform their rent reviews by comparing the rent you receive with rent paid for other similar properties in the area. If your property can justify a rent increase, the property manager will contact you to discuss it. If you agree to increase the rent, your property manager will send the required notice to the tenant. This process is completely automated, giving you peace of mind that you are not missing out on rental income.

If you are able to regularly increase your rent,

it will obviously benefit your cash flow. However, it is imperative that any rent increase is fair and can be justified. Many landlords who rent their investment property privately forget to regularly review their rent because they do not have a system to remind them. Then, when they do carry out a review, often after a period of several years, they have no idea how much the rent should be. They will often base an increase on unrelated factors such as what interest rates have been doing or whether council rates have gone up. These factors, while important to the landlord, have no bearing on the rent and are not justification for a rent increase. You should only increase rent on the basis of what the market is doing in your property's area.

Advertising

Whether you are advertising a property for rent or for sale, real-estate agencies receive better rates than people who advertise privately. This is simply because real-estate agencies advertise regularly, run large ads, and have accounts or subscriptions with advertising companies. Agencies can negotiate discounted rates substantially lower than a private person would pay, and the real-estate agency will pass these discounted rates on to their clients in full.

The two main forms of advertising are print media such as local newspapers, and internet based real-estate websites. But real-estate agencies' offices are another important source of advertising, and this represents another good reason to use a property manager. Most landlords will employ the services of a real-estate agency located in the same suburb as their rental property, and because of advertising through the agency, most tenants live in close proximity to their property manager's real-estate office.

Most tenants have a good relationship with their property manager and are familiar with their office because they signed the lease there, provided identification, paid a bond, collected keys and so on. Most tenants are happy to stay living in the same suburb year after year, particularly if they have children enrolled in local schools, and most tenants would be happy to rent another property through the same real-estate office. As a result, when a tenant needs to vacate a property and find a new one, the first place they go is to their property manager, who has a complete list in his or her office of all rental properties currently available and those that will be available in the near future.

Property managers also keep lists of prospective tenants who are looking for a suitable rental property, and records of good tenants they have had previous dealings with. This could mean not only that you get a great tenant, but also that you could save money by not needing to advertise.

In many cases, the property manager is the best form of advertising for a rental property. They know who is looking, who the good tenants are and what they want to rent. Many more properties are rented through property managers than through the other forms of advertising combined.

Choosing a tenant

Real-estate agencies require written applications from prospective tenants before considering if they are suitable for a particular property. When the agency receives the application, the property manager will obtain 100 points of identification from the prospective tenant, and carry out reference checks on matters including employment, credit history, and past rentals.

Property managers have access to several different databases they can use to check a tenant's rental history. Real-estate agencies subscribe to these databases to help them select the best tenant possible before accepting them into a property. The database lists tenants who have vacated a property with rent owing, and tenants who have damaged a property. Undesirable tenants can be added to the database by property managers, and while this is not a foolproof system, it is an important resource to help choose the best tenant and protect the landlord. Because property managers have access to this type of information, often bad tenants find their only option is to rent a property privately from a landlord. This is because landlords don't subscribe to the databases and often will not check references or look at a tenant's history. As a result, landlords renting privately are often left with rent owing and little recourse to recover the debt from the tenant.

In my experience, property managers in a particular neighbourhood or suburb also have an informal information-sharing arrangement that supplements the databases. Typically, property managers in an area know each other and will share information about bad tenants as a professional courtesy. They will offer a friendly warning to help another property manager avoid a potential disaster, with the expectation that they would be warned in return about other tenants. You cannot subscribe to this kind of resource, and although real-estate offices may deny that they share this information for reasons of privacy, the practice is alive and is very, very valuable to you as a landlord.

Condition reports

Understandably, most landlords are relieved when a tenant is found for their investment property and the lease agreement is signed. It is natural that the most prized document in a landlord's filing cabinet is the lease—but the next most important document is the condition report.

It is important to have a good condition report with supporting (and date-stamped!) photos. This is your proof of the condition your property was in when you let it to a tenant, against which any claim of damage to your property will be judged. A condition report should be prepared before the tenant moves in, and is intended as a reference point for checking that the condition of the property remains the same during the lease—with allowance for fair wear and tear.

Fair wear and tear is considered to be wear that a property would experience regardless of who was living there. For instance, carpets in high-traffic areas such as hallways will gradually wear thin and need replacing, regardless of who lives in the property. When a tenant vacates a property, a landlord will not be able to make a successful claim for compensation through the bond for worn carpets if the tribunal deems it was caused due to fair wear and tear.

As a property grows older and its fittings and fixtures grow older, things will naturally deteriorate and need to be replaced. This is to be expected, and it is the owner's responsibility. However, the owner can be compensated for any damage caused by the tenant beyond fair wear and tear. This is when a good, comprehensive condition report is vital.

By law, the tenant must be provided with a condition report before they move into a rental property. This will list every feature of the property, room by room. Some of the features will include:

- floor coverings
- window furnishings
- ceiling fans
- power points
- shelving
- air conditioner
- windows
- light fittings
- built-in robes
- TV aerial points
- heater

In the kitchen and bathroom, features such as wall and floor tiling, sinks, taps, vanity, bath, and shower will be listed.

The condition report will also list every defect or imperfection in the property, such as a stain on the carpet or a mark or blemish on a wall or ceiling.

In the state of Victoria, the tenant has three business days to return the condition report with their signature, acknowledging that they agree with the report—or they can add any additional defects that may have been missed. When the condition report is complete, it forms the basis against which the condition of the property will be measured.

If this condition report and six-monthly inspection reports are not completed correctly, accurately, or comprehensively, your chances of receiving compensation at a tribunal hearing for damage caused by a tenant are greatly diminished.

Bonds

Before a tenant moves into a rental property, they must pay a bond. They give this to the property manager, who is required to lodge the bond with the appropriate authority within a specified time frame.

The bond's purpose is to help ensure that a tenant looks after the rented property and pays their rent. When the tenant vacates the property, if there is any rent owing or any damage to the property beyond fair wear and tear, the landlord can make a claim against the tenant's bond to receive compensation.

A common misconception among landlords is that the bond belongs to them. This is not the case. The bond is held in trust on behalf of the tenant, and the bond belongs to the tenant at all times unless a claim is made at the end of the lease. If there is no claim made, the bond is returned in full to the tenant.

As with everything concerning rental properties, there are very specific rules and regulations about bonds that must be adhered to. Property managers know how to follow these procedures precisely and maintain good records that can be audited. Often landlords renting privately to a tenant run into trouble with bonds because they fail to get a bond, confuse the bond with rent paid in advance, or deposit the bond into their private bank account instead of lodging it with the appropriate authority. If the legislation is not followed correctly, fines and penalties can result.

Rent collection and accounting

Good, accurate bookkeeping is a cornerstone of any good business, and your investment property is a small business. So, if you are going to run your investment property correctly, you need to collect the rent, pay the outgoings including any maintenance and repairs, and have accurate records of all financial transactions relating to your investment.

If you can do this correctly, you can find out if your business can afford to grow by taking on more loans and buying more investment properties. The other reason good bookkeeping is essential is that you want to claim every tax deduction you are entitled to. If you miss an opportunity to claim, you could be missing out on money.

Real-estate agencies have very good accounting systems, because they are constantly receiving large amounts of money that do not belong to them. An estate agency receives rent on behalf of landlords, and sale deposits on behalf of sellers. This money is held in trust on behalf of the agencies' clients. There are very strict rules to follow in relation to trust accounts and their management, and severe penalties for those who don't follow them. Trust accounts of this kind are also independently audited each year to verify their accuracy.

As you would expect, a real-estate agency is also very good at collecting rent. They have an incentive to be, because they get a percentage of all rent they collect: this is their "management fee."

In addition to collecting rent, a real-estate agency is equally skilled at spending a landlord's money (with the landlord's consent) to pay for expenses relating to the property. These expenses can include repairs, maintenance, cleaning, gardening, council rates, water bills, and owners' corporation fees. The agency's services in this area can save landlords a lot of time, and also ensure that all bills are paid in a timely manner, avoiding late fees and additional charges.

At the end of the month, property managers send a statement to every landlord showing rent received and expenses paid. At the end of the financial year, they send a 12-month financial statement that summarises all income and all expenses. This makes bookkeeping easy for the landlord and ensures no tax deductions are missed. It can also save the landlord time and money, because at tax time they can simply pass on the 12-month financial statement to their tax agent, who will not then need to spend hours calculating income and expenses—the information will already be there.

Rent arrears

As I have mentioned, real-estate agencies are very good at collecting rent, because they get a percentage of the money. No rent collected means no fees for the agency.

When a tenant falls behind in their rent, there are correct procedures that must be followed and correct notices must be issued. All this is determined by legislation. Property managers have computer systems in place to monitor rent payments and notify them as soon as a tenant falls behind. If a tenant does fall behind, the property manager is trained to handle this situation and knows exactly what to do.

Often, landlords who rent their investment property privately do not handle this situation well. They aren't trained, find it uncomfortable to chase people for money, and want to avoid a confrontation with the tenant. But you cannot afford to be lenient or disorganised if rent is late, Unfortunately, if a tenant is shown leniency or procedures are not followed correctly, there is a very good chance that the tenant will become a habitual late payer and chasing rent money will be an ongoing problem. You can avoid this kind of problem by using a property manager.

Routine inspections

Legislation allows routine inspections to be carried out during the term of a rental lease. When a new lease is entered into, a property manager will enter the lease date into his or her computer and their software will automatically inform them when the inspection is due. These inspections are important as they allow the property manager and landlord to look through the property and ensure that it is being correctly looked after.

Maintenance

It is one of life's unfortunate realities that from time to time things will break or go wrong with a rental property. Property managers maintain lists of good, reliable tradespeople who they can call upon quickly to carry out repairs and maintenance. The property manager will take care to use only qualified, fully insured tradespeople, which protects the landlord if a catastrophe occurs that has something to do with the work.

The tradespeople in the property manager's contact list will usually have offered very competitive rates, much better than you would get privately, and the work is carried out promptly and efficiently. These tradespeople receive regular work from the property manager and will be paid on time. They want to keep their spot on the property manager's list, so they have an incentive to offer preferential rates and service.

Legislation and documentation

One of the many skills required to look after the lease on an investment property is a thorough understanding of legislation. Each state in Australia has its own residential tenancy act, and many other countries also have similarly complicated legislative environments.

Any lawyer will tell you that legislation can be a minefield for the unwitting. At times, a property manager needs to be a pseudo-lawyer. When you are working in a highly regulated area, such as real estate, it is important that you follow the letter of the law. The correct forms and notices must be used at all times, and the correct procedures and timings adhered to. One error or oversight can have devastating effects if you are ever required to attend a tribunal hearing to resolve a dispute.

As an example, I once witnessed a case brought to a tribunal hearing involving a tenant who was served a notice to vacate because he was well behind in his rent. That rent was owed was not in dispute: the tenant acknowledged he was well behind. However, the owner's case for evicting the tenant was thrown out because although they had served the tenant with the correct notice to vacate, the notice was not sent by registered post with the correct number of days allowed for postage.

I suspect that the tenant knew the notice had been served incorrectly because he had previously been served with similar notices on other properties. Even though that tenant was clearly in breach of the lease agreement, he won a stay of execution from being evicted, and the owner was taught the lesson that he must follow the law and comply with the *Residential Tenancies Act* and other legislation at all times.

As a result of this particular tribunal hearing, the owner had no other choice but to start the process again, serving a new notice to vacate, this time using registered post and allowing the required time. The good news for the owner was that after serving the new notice, the tenant did in fact leave the property within the required time. This was undoubtedly because the tenant knew the correct procedure had been followed the second time.

Similarly, I have seen instances where photos have been used in a tribunal hearing to show damage done to a property by a tenant, but the case has been dismissed because the photographs were not date-stamped.

Lots of small things can prevent you from getting the outcome you want or deserve in a hearing. Even though the tenant may be in breach of their lease, you may not necessarily get adequate compensation or justice in court. It makes sense to have a professional person representing you in a court of law or tribunal hearing because they are the experts, they are there to look after your best interests, and they have the best chance of getting you a favourable result.

Tenants tend to know their rights. Renting is a common and accepted living arrangement today, and many tenants move from one property to the next. As a result, many tenants have a good working understanding of the legislation as it applies to them. They are savvy enough to know when rent increases can be issued, how much notice is needed to inspect the property, when general inspections can and cannot be carried out, and how to go about reporting faults with a rental property. Whenever a tenant moves into a new rental property, they are given booklets explaining their rights and duties. If they need any clarification or help, they have access to advice services, and they can receive free legal assistance if they have any dispute or grievance. These advice services are only there to represent the tenant and the tenant's best interest, not those of landlords.

So, if you want to serve a notice to vacate, a rent increase, or any other documentation, you had better do it correctly and comply with legislation—otherwise you could be wasting your time. This is just one area in which it makes sense to use a property manager.

Legislation changes

As you would expect changes to legislation occur from time to time, including changes to required forms and notices. Real-estate agencies are informed of any changes through the industry bodies they are members of and subscriptions to information services. Often, as soon as new legislation is passed, training sessions are organised to help property managers implement new policies and procedures in their daily work practices.

If the new laws are not adhered to, penalties and fines apply. Ignorance is not recognised as an excuse. Property managers are your best insurance against changes to legislation. They will make sure your investment property is administered correctly and that you always comply with the law.

Preparing documents

The documentation involved with leasing and managing a rental property is extensive. As an example, when a tenant signs a lease agreement, some of the information they are provided with includes a copy of the lease (usually 20–30 pages), a condition report, bond lodgement forms and information, the agency's policies and procedures on things like rent arrears and routine inspections, a list of preferred trades-people and service providers, and a tenants' rights and information booklet.

Property managers need to have a myriad of forms and notices in their arsenal to ensure that the lease is managed correctly. Some of the forms and notices required under Victorian legislation include:

- lease agreement
- rent increase
- bond lodgement
- application to VCAT
- condition report
- breach notice
- bond claim
- notice of entry

Notices to vacate

- overdue rent
- repairs and renova-tions
- end of fixed-term lease
- occupation by landlord's family
- sub-letting
- successive breaches
- sale
- no specific reason
- illegal use
- change of use

By no means are these all of the forms and notices which can apply during the term of a lease. While determining which form applies to a specific situation may appear straightforward, the length of time given to the tenant changes from notice to notice.

Each state in Australia has their own variation of these forms and notices, and while their function and purpose will be essentially the same, the way in which you apply them will vary according to legislation in each state. Naturally, forms and notices, and the procedures and timings for submitting and serving them, will differ in other countries.

Of course, having the correct form or notice is one thing, but filling it in correctly is something else. At the end of the financial year, every person in Australia can pick up a free copy of the Australian Tax Pack and do their taxes themselves, but unless you are familiar with the pack it can be a daunting and very time-consuming process. Because of this, many people use a trained tax agent, while many of those who persevere and tackle the tax pack themselves will fail to fill it in correctly.

Property managers are trained to know how and when to use particular forms and notices in accordance with legislation, and how to complete all documentation correctly.

Lease renewals

When a lease expires, the tenant does not have to vacate the property unless they are served with the prescribed notices in accordance with the legislation. If the tenant remains in the property, the lease changes from a *fixed* lease to a *periodic* or *month-to-month* lease. All of the conditions of the original lease stay in place, so the day-to-day management of the rental property is unaffected. This situation could be desirable for the landlord if they are thinking of selling the property in the near future.

When a lease is periodic, a notice can be served on the tenants at any time informing them that vacant possession is required. This is not the case when the lease is for a fixed period. If the property is sold with a fixed lease, the buyer must comply with the existing lease. But if the landlord has no intention of selling their investment property, a fixed lease offers greater protection for the tenant and landlord. The major advantage for the landlord is that if the tenant breaks the lease and vacates the property, the tenant still has to pay the rent until a new suitable tenant is found. The advantage with a fixed lease for the tenant is security of tenure and the peace of mind that comes with it.

Often, when a landlord rents their property privately, they forget to renew a lease at the end of the fixed period. This is probably because, to all outward appearances, nothing has changed. The landlord may even be unaware that the lease has expired. If the property is being managed by a real-estate agency, the property manager will contact the landlord at the end of the lease and find out what their intentions are concerning the property, including whether they would like a lease renewal.

As I have mentioned, if the lease is renewed, this gives the landlord a form of income protection. The other consideration is that in the majority of cases, if a fixed lease is broken, landlord insurance offers a greater level of protection and you can make a larger claim.

Tribunal appearances

Unless you are a legal eagle, you are probably unfamiliar with tribunal and court hearings, and the thought of attending a hearing, let alone addressing one, would be a daunting prospect. It is also very time-consuming. Unfortunately, one of the occupational hazards of being a property manager is that at some point in time you will need to attend a tribunal hearing and give evidence. As a result, property managers are thoroughly versed in what to do at a hearing, how to address the hearing, and the etiquette involved. A property manager is certainly a lot cheaper than a lawyer, and a whole lot better than representing yourself as a novice landlord.

Landlord insurance

I mentioned that having a qualified property manager is just like having a comprehensive insurance policy. But while a property manager can save you from a lot of pitfalls, there is no substitute for actual insurance.

In *How to Buy Unlimited Investment Properties*, I wrote about the importance of insurances, including home and contents insurance, landlord insurance, private health cover, death cover, income protection insurance, total temporary disability, and total permanent disability insurances. As a result, I will not expand on this topic greatly, except to reiterate my opinion that landlord insurance is an absolute must if you own an investment property.

Some of the things covered in a landlord insurance policy are:

- damage caused to the property by the tenant
- lost rent due to damage caused by the tenant

- rent default due to a tenant breaking a lease
- theft
- legal expenses

If something goes wrong with your investment property due to the tenant, then landlord insurance can save you from a serious financial burden.

If you do need to lodge an insurance claim, the insurance company will request a copy of the rental lease, bond lodgement forms, and condition reports. If the landlord has not complied with legislation, or is in breach of the lease, the claim may not be approved.

Property managers can be of enormous help when making an insurance claim. In my experience, when a claim is made under landlord insurance, the property manager has provided the insurance company with all the documentation including proof of claim, has shown the insurance assessor through the property, and generally facilitated everything to do with and in support of the claim.

Finally, the cost for landlord insurance is nominal and can be claimed as a tax deduction. There is no good reason not to have it.

A final note

The last comment I would like to make on this subject is to keep the costs of employing a property manager in perspective. Whenever a landlord says to me, "I will manage my own rental property," my immediate reaction is, "Why would anyone want to do that?" Typically the answer is, "To save a few dollars."

A fully qualified property manager will cost you 5–7% of the gross rent. So, if your investment property is rented for $500 per week, the management fees will cost you $25–35 per week. Over a full year, this will add up to between $1,300–1,820 of the $26,000 total rent collected for the year.

I agree that, on the surface, this can appear to be a reasonable amount of money—but keep it in perspective! How hard are you prepared to work for $1,300–1,820?

It is true a property manager will spend 90% of their time and effort looking after problems involving 10% of their management portfolio, but your property could be in that 10%. It is also true that if you have a great long-term tenant who is taking exceptional care of your property, the management of your property is made easier. But the flipside is that to ensure it remains a great property to manage, it must still be managed correctly. Otherwise, it is very easy for small things to go off the rails and quickly become a major problem.

Of course, you can't know if your next tenant will be great, or a great big pain in your backside. Similarly, you don't know if your house is going to burn down, but you still take out insurance. You might look back at the year past and think about the money you could have saved if you managed your own investment property, cancelled your home and car insurance, and got rid of your private health insurance—but what would it have cost you in sleepless nights and peace of mind?

The widely recognised real-estate industry standard for property managers is that they need to manage 150–200 properties each to make it financially viable for the real-estate agency. This may seem like a lot of properties, but it needs to take into account the property manager's wage, travel expenses, continual professional development and training costs, superannuation, phone, subscriptions, postage, stationery, computer software, and so on. A property manager cannot survive on a management portfolio of 50 or even 100 properties. It just is not financially viable. If you are managing your own investment portfolio, is it really worth the trouble?

Finally, putting money aside, having a property manager means you do not have to stress, because—believe me—they will stress for you. Every time we experience a sudden change in temperature, property managers lose sleep. They know that when the weather turns cold for the first time that year, they will be inundated with calls from tenants complaining that their heater is not working and they want it fixed immediately. When the first hot spell of summer arrives, all the tenants will want their air-conditioning working at the same time. And in extreme weather conditions like severe storms or gale-force winds, a property manager's stress levels go off the charts.

When anything goes wrong with your investment property, your property manager is the first person the tenant calls. Even if the roof has just blown off your property, or a tree has fallen through it, the tenant won't call emergency services first: they will call their faithful, reliable, sleep-deprived property manager.

With a property manager acting as your intermediary, you don't need to worry about phone calls in the middle of the night saying, "roof tiles have blown off," or "I have locked myself out of the house; can you let me back in?" Sure—at times, managing a rental property can *appear* easy, but it typically isn't. I never manage my own rental properties, even though I know I can do what's required. I gladly choose to hand over the management of all my rental properties to a property manager. This allows me to relax and focus on more pleasurable pursuits, like writing this book.

Summary

- Employing the services of a fully qualified property manager will cost you 5–7% of gross rent.
- While it may seem that you could save money by managing your property yourself, employing the services of a good property manager through a real-estate agency will save you time and stress. In the long-term, it is also likely to save you more money than you paid in fees.
- A good property manager will have great communication skills, act as a mediator and interpreter between landlord and tenant, and have an exhaustive knowledge of relevant legislation.
- Property managers will help you in the following areas:
    - Determining the correct rent and conducting reviews to make sure that you can increase rents in line with the market.
    - Advertising your property to prospective tenants in relevant media as well as through the

real-estate agency office.

- Choosing the right tenant, including checking references and accessing tenant information databases available only to property managers.
- Collecting and lodging bonds correctly.
- Preparing the condition report when a new tenant is about to move in.
- Conducting routine inspections to make sure the property is being looked after.
- Collecting and accounting for rent, including missed payments.
- Issuing monthly and yearly reports of income and expenses relating to properties they manage. These reports will help you manage your portfolio effectively, and ease preparation of your tax returns.
- Arranging timely maintenance by good, reliable, and cost-effective tradespeople, where necessary.
- Issuing correct forms and notices, and following other procedures, with the correct timing.
- Renewing leases.
- Appearing at tribunal hearings if required.

• Landlord insurance can protect you from a range of adverse events, including damage caused by the tenant, rent default due to a tenant breaking a lease, theft, and legal expenses. It can save you serious money if something goes wrong, the cost is nominal, and it can be claimed as a tax deduction. There is no good reason not to have it.

8. Top 10 rules to remember

In *How to Buy Unlimited Investment Properties*, I in-cluded a list of 10 top rules to remember. I believe that these are crucial to ensure your success. In that list, I challenged readers to question some long-held views like "rent money is dead money" and "debt is bad." I also discussed why you should expect the worst, how to listen and take advice from people who have achieved what you want to achieve, the importance of appearing confident and relaxed when negotiating, not being miserly, and having clearly defined goals.

I also mentioned that I learn a little bit more every time I purchase a property and add to my list of rules as I go. These rules come from my personal experi-ences, and as a result some rules may seem obvious to some readers, while others will feel that I have omitted a more important rule. For this reason, I en-courage you to modify or add to the rules I have compiled. Through your own experience, you will gradually form your own list of the top 10 rules to remember when investing in property.

The rules I have provided here don't replace those I listed in my first book—they are simply additional rules. More specifically, these are the rules that sprang to mind when I was considering the advice I'd give to someone who not only wanted to buy unlimited investment properties, but who did so with the aim to *retire in 10 years*, using the strategies I have described.

Whatever your goal as an investor, all of these rules will be important to you at some point when you are building your investment portfolio.

1. It takes money to make money

I have given this well-known saying a lot of thought, probably because I first heard it when I was a teenager.

The idea that it takes money to make money is disconcerting to someone who doesn't have any, or has very little. As a teenager, I certainly didn't have a lot of money, but I knew I needed it and wanted it.

If you believe this saying, it could be paralysing. What's the point in trying to make money if you don't have any to begin with? Wouldn't you be wasting your time?

But surely, you couldn't be wasting your time—we've all heard stories about battlers who made millions from nothing. In fact, I recently read a magazine article that said that 80% of all millionaires are self-made. Just look at people like Mark Zuckerberg, who is credited with starting Facebook; Sir Richard Branson, who created Virgin Airlines among many other brands; and Frank Lowy, who escaped death at the hands of the Nazis as a teenager before eventually coming to Australia, where he started the multi-billion-dollar Westfield shopping-mall empire. These people are an inspiration for anyone who believes they can make their own fortune.

But what of the statistics that show in countries like Australia and America, where capitalism is the way of life, the middle class is disappearing and the chasm between the haves and have-nots is growing—that the rich are getting richer and the poor are getting poorer? Isn't it true that nearly all the wealth in the world, over 80% of it, is controlled by only 20% of the population?

Having given the statement, "it takes money to make money," plenty of thought over the years, and from my own personal experiences dealing with finance companies, I've come to believe that while it is not *necessarily* true that you need to have money to make money, it certainly helps. The more money you have, the more negotiating power you have, and the better a deal you can strike for yourself.

One example of this is glaringly obvious every

time you step into a bank branch and look at the signs advertising term deposits. If you are considering using a term deposit, you will get a higher return if you invest more money. So, the more money you have to invest, the higher the interest rate you will receive and the more money you will make. Unfortunately, if you are a battler with less to invest, you will get a lower interest rate.

Another example is the interest rate you will be charged on a loan. The larger the loan, the more the banks want your business and the lower the rates they will charge you. If you consolidate loans into one larger loan and shop around with different lenders, you will be able to secure a better deal than if you had smaller loans with multiple lenders.

By claiming that it is easier to make money if you already have money, I don't mean to depress anyone. I mention it to point out that making money gets easier the more you do it. Just like training for a sport, the more you do it, the better you become and the easier it is. The crucial component is that you must be financially literate, as I discussed in Chapter 4. If you ask any self-made millionaire, they will tell you that the first million dollars was the hardest to make, and every million dollars after that became easier and easier.

The more important aspect of this rule is that

you understand and accept this is the way things work. If you accept this, you can start to think of ways to make the system work for your benefit. As I explained in *How to Buy Unlimited Investment Properties*, I formed syndicates to give me greater buying power. Forming syndicates enabled me to negotiate larger discounts for buying properties in bulk, which I would not have been able to do had I purchased only a single property. It also allowed me to negotiate better loans from the bank.

I know people who have joined similar groups and now buy shares in bulk to save on brokerage fees. I also know people, including myself, who have collectively pooled their money and invested in term deposits to take advantage of higher interest rate returns. It may seem trivial to go to this effort just to get an extra 0.5% or 1% return on your investment. But if you do this multiple times, the extra bit of interest you earn can add up to a large sum of money. The money could pay for your next holiday, or it could make your life a bit easier. The choice is yours. Self-made millionaires and people who are financially literate make sure that they make their money work for them, and that they receive every advantage they are entitled to.

2. Don't be a slumlord—keep your properties in good repair

Thanks largely to the media, I am sure that most people have read or heard a horror story involving a tenant destroying a rental property. It is true that these things happen occasionally, but unfortunately, because of the way these stories are often reported, it can create an image of all tenants as terrible people who aren't fit to live in or look after another person's property. This is unfair, and as a whole, tenants often get a bad rap.

These horror stories are rare, and need to be kept in perspective. While there are some terrible tenants, the overwhelming majority are excellent. Consider this: approximately one third of all properties are rented, another third are owned outright by the occupants, and the remaining third are mortgaged and being paid off by the occupants. If the majority of homes currently being rented had bad tenants, the evidence would be clear for all to see each time you drive through your neighbourhood. Most tenants take excellent care of the home they live in, but unfortunately, a small minority spoils the reputation of the rest.

By contrast, landlords rarely attract bad media coverage—but terrible landlords definitely exist.

There are just as many terrible landlords as terrible tenants. There are registers that attempt to protect landlords from undesirable tenants, but none warning prospective tenants who the bad landlords are.

A bad landlord is someone who will not carry out any repairs or maintenance, even minor ones, on their investment property even after the tenant makes repeated requests. But at the same time, these landlords still insist on receiving rent each week, and they demand the tenant looks after the property. I doubt these landlords would tolerate the same defects in their own home, where they would not hesitate to carry out repairs.

You want your property portfolio to be a well-oiled business, and the most crucial ingredient in any such business is the people that work in it. Your goal should be to treat them with respect, keep them happy, and retain them for as long as possible.

The same thinking should apply to your tenants. These people also ensure your business runs smoothly, by paying you rent. Ideally, your tenants won't vacate every 12 months, but will stay long term. By having a long-term tenant, you avoid the possibility of your investment property sitting vacant with no rental income, and you avoid costs like having to advertise for a new tenant and paying letting fees to the estate agent.

Keeping your properties in good condition is one thing that will keep your tenants happy. As a responsible landlord, whenever you receive a request for a repair, you should have it fixed. When a tenant enters into a lease agreement, they are entitled to assume that everything in the property is in perfect working order. If a prospective tenant sees an alarm, dishwasher, heater, air conditioner, light, cooking appliance, etc., they are within their rights to assume it works, unless specifically told otherwise. If something breaks down after the tenant moves in, it is not only reasonable to expect that the landlord repairs or replaces it—it is actually mandatory. After all, that item is part of the property that the tenant pays rent for.

There is, however, a distinction between repairs and requests for improvements to be made to the property. If a tenant makes a request for something that was not previously in the property, you have a choice between spending the money or leaving it as is. If you decide to provide the requested item, you are within your rights to request more rent.

As an example, I once I had a request from a tenant to install an air-conditioner into an investment property, months after the tenant had moved in. I gladly agreed to install air conditioning after the tenants agreed to extend the lease by a further 12 months and we increased the rent by $15 per week. The extra rent I received helped pay for the air conditioning, for which I also claimed depreciation in my tax return.

The air-conditioning is an improvement to my property, and should hopefully increase its value. Even more fortunately, the tenants who requested the air conditioning still rent the same property from me 7 years later. I know many landlords who have tenants that have been in the same property for over 10 years, as I do myself. Some people will say this is just good luck, and I agree that can play a part, but the same landlords consistently attract long-term tenants, and good management plays a more important role.

The best time to carry out minor repairs and improvements to your property is between one tenant moving out and another moving in. If your investment is being taken care of by a property manager, they will inspect it and complete a condition report, but you should also visit the property and look for defects. The property manager will be looking for obvious things like whether the tenant has damaged the property or left it dirty or untidy, and if they have removed all their belongings?

You should keep in mind that a tenant can vacate a property and leave it perfect *allowing for fair wear and tear*. This might mean that it was left in perfect condition but—oops, there is a mark on the entry wall from moving furniture. You might not be able to deduct money from the tenant's bond for this, but you should be asking yourself, Is my property fit to live in? Is it well presented? Can I make any improvements? Would *I* live here?

If there are marks on the walls, they should be cleaned or painted. Check that smoke detectors, tiles, and toilet-roll holders are properly fixed in place, that curtains are hanging correctly, taps are not dripping, and all globes in light fittings are working. Outside, make sure the lawns are mown and edged, and that garden beds are weeded.

Lots of small defects can be easily attended to while there is no one living in the property. If you don't attend to them when you have the chance, they can accumulate until the whole property looks shabby, unloved, and neglected. Touch-up painting is a perfect example of a small job that can have an enormous effect on the way your property looks and how tenants will treat it. If the walls in your investment property start out unblemished, the next tenant will take greater care to keep them that way, because they know any mark on a wall will be attributed to them. On the other hand, if the walls are already covered in marks and cracks, there will be no way to tell what an outgoing tenant is responsible for, and they will have no reason to take special care to avoid making things worse.

In short, by taking care of your investment and pride in the way it is presented, you will be more likely to attract a tenant who will take good care of that property. You can also demand a better rent, and as a result, a larger bond. Larger bonds ensure better tenants, because tenants want their bond back when they vacate your property. A bond is usually equivalent to one month's rent, and as rents increase, so do bonds, which are now often in excess of $2,000. When the bond is high, so is the tenant's desire to get their money back. As a result, they will respect your property and treat it like it was their own home.

3. You can make a difference

Obviously, I like investing in real estate. I believe there are many advantages to this type of investment, and one of my favourites is that *you can make a difference*, which you often cannot do when you invest in other asset classes.

Most investors put their faith and hard-earned money in either real estate or shares. In my opinion, one of the problems with shares is the investor's inability to affect the share price or the dividend. With shares, you adopt an entirely passive position and can only watch as other people make decisions concerning your investment. If the share price falls, you cannot just drop into the company and change the situation, or even influence the situation slightly. You cannot, as a rule, volunteer your time or expertise, and work at the company in exchange for a climbing share price. No amount of effort on your part will make any difference.

Investing in shares is like placing a bet on a horse. You can carry out research and make an educated decision about which horse (or company) will be the better performer, but once you have placed your bet, you can only sit back and watch the outcome.

One of the exciting things about investing in real estate, as distinct from shares, is that you can play an active role and make a difference. There are hundreds of ways you can add value to your property, which will increase your rental income and your property's value. These can be as small as cleaning walls and surfaces, mowing the lawn, or pulling a weed out of the garden bed. You don't need to be Jamie Durie and do a *Backyard Blitz*, or carry out large-scale renovations—even the smallest improvements help the property.

Every improvement you make has an effect, enhance the appearance of your property and increasing its appeal to buyers. This will help create competition among buyers, lead to a quicker sale, and get you a better price. If you don't want to sell your property, you can capitalise on the increased property value by going to your lender and refinancing, which you cannot do with most other investments. By getting a new, larger loan, you can free up some of the increased equity you have in the property.

Carrying out small improvements on your property may not necessarily translate into tens of thousands of dollars more in your pocket, but it will help increase the value of your investment. If you do decide to sell, even the smallest improvements will help you achieve a better price and sell your property quicker, saving on marketing costs.

When you invest in real estate, you *can* take an entirely passive position and let natural market forces run their course. But if you take an interest in your investment property, you will find there are many, many ways that you can make a small or even a big difference. The choice is yours.

4. Be real-estate savvy

Real estate has become very fashionable thanks to the large number of television programs and magazines dedicated to all things real-estate, including things like renovations and auctions. As a result, there are many people keenly interested in buying, renovating, and selling property.

Television shows and magazines are a great source of information about the latest trends, colour schemes, innovations, and so on. But another easy way to keep yourself informed is to visit your local display homes.

Building companies invest large sums of money to make sure their display homes are finished, landscaped, and presented to the highest standard. These homes are the company's flagships: they represent the company and are intended to generate lots of buyer enquiries and interest, leading to new building contracts and, eventually, homes.

To try stay one step ahead of the competition, building companies employ interior designers and fashion consultants to make sure that no detail, however minor, is overlooked. The display homes feature the latest in home furnishings, soft music plays, and the dinner table is set as though waiting for guests to arrive. The attention to detail is outstanding. Although you may not present your property to display-home standards when you sell, you can still take many great ideas from display homes to ensure that you appeal to as many potential buyers as possible.

Another benefit to visiting a display home is that the experience is more tactile than flicking through a magazine or watching images on a television. You use more senses when you physically walk through a property. You can feel the tiles and wallpaper to check if they are textured, and you can hear the music playing and smell the flowers or potpourri placed throughout the home. The experience, overall, is far more engaging—but the most important thing is that after visiting a display village you will walk away with a sense of what is trendy and what buyers are looking for and expecting in their next home.

If you are real-estate savvy and can replicate some of the display-home colour schemes, finishes, and décor in your own property, you will create far greater buyer appeal and achieve a better sale price.

5. Look forward, never back

Be content and secure in the knowledge that your past decisions were the best you could make for yourself and your family based on all the knowledge and information you had at the time.

This doesn't mean we should ignore the past. We should learn from it, particularly our failures. History is the best teacher, and our life experiences the best lesson. But dwelling on what could have or should have been is counterproductive.

Particularly when it comes to real estate, people often look back and reminisce about the property they could have bought for a fraction of its current value, or they fixate on the property they sold for significantly less than what it is worth today.

You will get no pleasure or benefit from dwelling on what could have or should have been.

6. Be inspired

Inspiration can come to us in the most unlikely forms, at the most peculiar times. Keep an open mind and allow yourself to be inspired. Don't dismiss an idea just because you did not think of it yourself, or because you think it is too simple or too good to be true. Don't be cynical: the world is full of cynics and we don't need any more.

I am not advocating that you make judgments on blind faith alone. By all means, be objective, and use your intellect to investigate. Question and challenge ideas, but do so with an open mind. You might be surprised at the outcome.

I hope that I have inspired some readers to think about their current financial position, where they want to be in 10 years, what they are doing to reach their goals in 10 years or sooner, and, if necessary to make plans to reach their goals. I was inspired to write this book by my editor, family, and friends, and I am grateful for that.

Inspiration isn't just about making money. It's involved in every aspect of our lives. You may have watched a reality TV show and been inspired to take dancing lessons or lose weight, you may have been inspired to holiday in an exotic location after watching a travel show, or your children may have inspired you to become a fitter, better person. We are inspired by family, friends, acquaintances, spouses, children, colleges, peers, strangers, celebrities, teachers and many, many other people, every day. Through your actions, your decisions, and by telling your story you inspire people around you. You choose whether or not that inspiration is positive or negative.

If you don't keep an open mind, or allow negative thoughts to fester, you cannot be inspired. In our technological age, with unlimited access to information, we can find inspirational stories everywhere. There are amazing stories of ordinary people accomplishing incredible feats. For instance, though we still have not found a cure for cancer, there are stories of individuals who have survived and overcome cancer, defying all medical odds.

Don't tell yourself or anyone else that something is impossible: allow yourself and others the opportunity to be inspired.

7. Know that real estate is forgiving

Even if you bought the worst property, in the worst location, at the worst time, the chances are still excellent that over time the property will still increase in value. History has proven that over a long period, property is possibly the most forgiving type of investment. Unlike other types of investments, a property's value never disappears or drops to zero. In case a disaster does occur, there are numerous insurances that can cover you against most types of loss. This gives certainty and comfort to investors, and is one reason why many wealthy people hold vast quantities of money in real estate. Most other investment classes are subject to much greater risk of loss.

There is also nothing difficult or complicated about investing in property. There's typically no secrets or information being withheld from you. Anyone can invest in real estate; it is relatively straight forward.

Depending on your personal financial circumstances, you can invest as much or as little as you like. Because the value of properties consistently grows, banks are willing to loan money for investment properties. Sometimes they are even prepared to lend more than a property is worth, because they are confident that the property will continue to grow in value.

As I have previously mentioned, residential property in Australia's major capital cities has historically increased in value by an average of around 7% per annum. This growth has been reliable over time and consistently adds to the investor's wealth. At this rate of growth, a property will double in value about every 10 years. When this capital growth is combined with rental increases, the return on investment property is tremendous, and regularly outperforms other asset classes.

Often, the reason we choose to do the same thing day after day is fear. We may not openly acknowledge this because it would make us feel embarrassed or inadequate. You may have heard the saying, "the definition of insanity is to do the same thing time after time and expect a different result." If you have avoided investing in property out of fear, but still not achieved the level of wealth you aspire to, it is possible that your circumstances will never change unless you first change your course of action.

Presumably, one of the reasons you are reading

this book is that you want to improve your financial position. If so, you have nothing to fear: even if you buy the wrong property, so long as you are patient and hold onto it, over time it will most likely increase in value even if you do nothing to it. Real estate is very forgiving.

8. Practice

They say practice makes perfect. This saying alone can drive us to keep trying the same thing over until we get it right. We can see this very easily in sports: the desire and need to kick or hit a ball perfectly drives sportspeople to practice the same action over and over, week after week. Of course, no matter how many times a sportsperson practices they will never have a perfect game. That is why in football we record "clangers" and "efficiency rates," and in tennis the number of "unforced errors," to identify how many mistakes players make.

With this information, and perhaps a quote from Andre Agassi—"if you don't practice, you don't deserve to win"—the sportsperson will turn up at their next training session and repeat the same drills as the day before, in the hope that they will approach perfect performance.

The reason I mention this is because life is one big practice session. Every time you have a meeting, discussion, debate, or negotiation, you are practicing for your *next* meeting, discussion, debate or negotiation. Every time you do these things, you get better: you run a better meeting, you speak more eloquently, debate more confidently, and negotiate more successfully.

When you start on your journey to acquiring your investment property portfolio, you begin tentatively, are nervous about auctions and unsure about finance, and you question whether you have done enough due diligence. When you begin, there is a steep learning curve. Many things seem difficult and will take you out of your comfort zone, like bidding at an auction or negotiating to buy multiple properties. But once you have started and you get practice, after a while everything will become second nature, just like a sportsperson kicking a ball.

Without consciously thinking about it, we practice every day in everything we do. I now have two adorable children, and every day I practice becoming a better parent in the hope that one day I will be perfect—but I also know I am not, and it is important to keep that perspective. I have called hundreds of auctions, but I have never called the *perfect* auction and know I never will. There is always room to improve.

I am my own harshest critic, and I will always think that I could have done something better, but I keep practicing and hopefully improving. Whatever the task is, big or small, we are continuously practicing and becoming better at it.

With practice, your confidence will grow, the tasks you once dreaded will no longer seem that difficult, and with hindsight you will wonder why you hesitated. All you needed to do was practice—and you do that every day of your life.

9. Share your knowledge and reap the rewards

In *How to Buy Unlimited Investment Properties*, I describe techniques you can use to help you negotiate. I also explain the importance of using pauses and receiving more information than you give. But not everything to do with real-estate investing is a negotiation. You don't need to guard information to get an advantage over other investors. There are plenty of properties for all of us, and no one who wants to start buying investment properties or add to their portfolio is going to miss out.

I have previously acknowledged that many people have helped me along the way with property investing, and I hope that I have helped people with their investments in turn. Likewise, I have also mentioned the help you can receive by working in a team, group, or syndicate where you can brainstorm about ideas and problems.

Openly discussing your experiences and ideas about property investing with other investors can be greatly beneficial for everyone. If you share information, you will also receive information. However long I have been involved with real estate, I am still constantly learning more.

Other investors are a great source of information. Even if they have less experience than you, or own fewer properties, they may have recently experienced something you are unfamiliar with. They could have come across changes to legislation, depreciation, or banking practices, or they might be using strategies you have not considered, like buying properties using self-managed super funds or investing in commercial property. Maybe they have received rebates you've never applied for, for something like installing solar panels or improving a property's energy efficiency. Because so many things are constantly changing, you should never be arrogant and think that you know everything.

Most people I have asked for advice or help have been extremely generous with their time and knowledge, and I have benefited greatly from it. All I had to do was ask the question.

There are many investors clubs and the like that have been formed for people to get together and share ideas and information. Whether these are organised clubs, syndicates, or just a few like-minded people getting together, they can be a huge help and give you the encouragement and confidence to take the next step. You just need to be open-minded and prepared to share experiences and information so that you can also reap the rewards.

10. Just do it

This is the last message I wish to impart in this book, and I hope it is the most lasting. There are thousands of books out there that offer inspirational slogans, practices, and insights, some of them subtle and profound. But of them all, the simplest is the most important:

JUST DO IT!

As I have mentioned, I have read many books and attended many seminars on property investment, goal setting, motivation, self-improvement, and making money, and I have friends whose bookshelves are crammed with this type of literature. I have met people who have literally walked on burning coals in the hope of proving the power of mind over matter. In many cases, they received third degree burns on the soles of their feet.

The message of many self-help style books is that focusing your desires, setting goals, writing them down and reading them every morning and evening, and visualising your path, is the key to success. In essence, these books say that thinking rich will make you rich.

In my opinion, no matter how hard you think about money, how much you wish for it, dream about it, or desire it, you will not magically become rich. In saying this, I have most likely enraged some motivational gurus. But wishing for something alone cannot make it real. If that were true, every little boy would grow up to be a star athlete and play sport for a living, and every little girl would become a pop star or a princess.

There are people who would have you believe that they simply thought about getting rich and the money materialised. Likewise, I am sure that there are people who believe that they were abducted by aliens and taken to the mother ship. These people could be right, and I don't mean to debate the point. Take it as solely my opinion if you like: growing rich will not come to you merely because you think about it.

If it is that easy, why are so many people poor? Why do so many struggle to pay bills, or toil at a job they dislike? And why do so many people put off doing the things they really want to do? Surely, just thinking about doing something is not enough.

What ultimately stands in most people's way is a lack of **ACTION**. It is the fundamental difference between the haves and have-nots. Throughout my life, during my childhood, school years, and work life, I have known "gonna's." These people are always "gonna" do something, like make a million dollars, quit smoking, be famous, be a star actor, lose 30 kilograms, travel the world, or lead the country. You have undoubtedly met these people, too. They come from all walks of life, all nations and religions. They are male and female, young and old. What they all have in common is that their dreams never come true, because they never do anything about them.

I don't want to be a dream killer. In fact, dreams are vital: an essential ingredient in what drives us, and an intrinsic part of who we are. I hope my own children have big dreams, and I hope that all of their dreams come true. For that to happen, they will have to understand that dreams, desires, and wishes are catalysts for change, but they do not *result* in change unless **action** is taken to make it happen.

If you only dream of growing rich, I fear that you will not change your current situation, and the status quo will continue.

To change your financial position for the better, you must take **action**. The time to only think about it has passed. Stop procrastinating and **just do it**. Don't expect that your financial circumstances will improve merely because you desire or dream of improvement. **You must take action.**

So many self-help books don't tell you where to start. They don't give you a road map, and as the reader, you can end up spending too much time looking inward when you should be looking at all the opportunities which are passing you by. I've often read such books myself, felt a warm, fuzzy feeling inside and felt empowered to do something, but I have not then known what I should do next. Like the high from a drug, this feeling fades in the weeks and months that follow, and then I start looking for another pick-me-up.

I don't want this to happen to you. So in the next, final chapter of this book, I will tell you *exactly what to do next if you want to get rich.*

Summary

1. *It takes money to make money.* There are enough stories of self-made millionaires that no one should be discouraged from pursuing wealth because they currently lack it. But the adage is true, and the more money you have, the greater your negotiating power and the more you have to build on.

2. *Don't be a slumlord—keep your properties in good repair.* Taking care of your investment and taking pride in how your properties are presented will attract better tenants who take better care of your assets.

3. *You can make a difference.* One of the most exciting things about investing in real estate is that your own effort can increase the value of your investment, something you don't get to experience when investing in most other asset classes.

4. *Be real-estate savvy.* Property developers employ interior designers and trend consultants to stay ahead of the market and the competition. Be similarly savvy: pay attention to detail.

5. *Look forward, never back.* History and life experience are the best teachers. Don't dwell on things you could have done better or opportunities you may have missed. Focus on using what you've

learned to do better and better.

6. *Inspiration.* Never dismiss ideas just because you didn't think of them or because they seem too simple or too good to be true. Keep an open mind and allow yourself to be inspired.

7. *Real estate is forgiving.* Investing in property is simple. With diligence, anyone can learn to do it skilfully. Property values grow consistently. There is nothing difficult or complicated about investing in property. Anyone can invest in real estate and it is relatively straightforward. Banks are willing to loan money for investment properties because they know their value will consistently grow. Even if you buy the "wrong" property, it is still likely to increase in value if you are patient and hold on to it.

8. *Practice.* If you start investing in property today, over time your confidence will grow, tasks you once dreaded will no longer seem difficult, and you will make better investment decisions.

9. *Share your knowledge and reap the rewards.* Share your experiences and knowledge with other investors, and they will share it with you. Not only will this aid you in your investment efforts, but clubs, syndicates and the like are also a great source of community and encouragement.

10. *Just do it.* Dreams and desires, and wishes are all

catalysts for change, but simply wishing for things has no magic power. You will only see change and results if you take action to make things happen. Start taking practical steps now to achieve your goals.

9. Exactly what to do next if you want to get rich

Step 1. Buy an investment property

Here, and in my first book, *How to Buy Unlimited Investment Properties,* I've explained what attributes you should be looking for in your investment property and where you should look. The next thing to do is buy one.

As you're setting out, remember that research is the key. Carry out due diligence and make sure that you are not paying too much for your investment. If you are going to sell an investment property after owning it for only a short time (a couple of years), most of your profit will come from the price you paid for the property not the sale price, which the real-estate market will determine. If you can buy the property at a discount to its intrinsic value, you have a good chance of making a profit when selling.

Buy an investment property within the next three months. You need to set a time limit. Make this commitment right now! Believe in yourself: you

243

are ready. It's not an unrealistic time frame. You don't need to buy a property by the close of business tomorrow, but you do need to do it as soon as you reasonably can.

Three months is enough time to carry out market research and complete your due diligence. Don't make excuses or procrastinate any longer. This is the first step to your financial freedom. Whatever today's date happens to be, add three months. It will not take you any longer than 11–12 weeks of research to become an expert on property prices in a particular area.

When you have found a suitable property, buy it, but make sure you add a "subject to bank finance" clause in the contract. Note that this will prevent you from buying a property at auction, because under the terms of an auction, all offers must be unconditional. The subject to bank finance clause is your ultimate safety net. If you have overcommitted and cannot afford the property, the bank will reject your loan application and consequently, the contract you have signed to buy the property will not proceed. Any money you have paid to the real-estate agent will be refunded in full. The other benefit of a subject to bank finance clause is that as part of the approval process, the bank will independently assess the value of the property you wish to buy. This is usually done by a sworn valuer on behalf of the bank. The process gives you further peace of mind because if the property you are buying is valued at less than the price you have offered, the loan will be declined.

If you can buy a property within the next three months, you are on your way. I congratulate you. If you try to buy an investment property and fail because the bank would not provide you with finance, look at the experience as practice for your next attempt. Next time, you will do better.

Remember that you are infinitely better off for trying to do something and failing than those who have tried nothing and succeeded. If you tried and failed, you are closer to succeeding next time. You should consider the "subject to bank finance" clause absolutely non-negotiable. Treat it as mandatory; it *must* be included in the purchase contract. This clause is your ultimate get-out-of-jail card. If you have overcommitted and cannot afford to buy the property, any money paid by you will be fully refunded and the experience should not cost you anything other than your time.

Whether or not you succeed or fail, you will have taken **action**, which is commendable. If you need any further encouragement or help, ask people that already own investment properties or contact me personally. I have included my contact details at the back of this book, and I would love to hear from readers about their experiences.

Step 2. After 12–18 months, buy another investment property

Incredibly, most investors forget or neglect this most fundamental and important step. Amazingly, the vast majority of investors own only one investment property. According to RP Data (now CoreLogic) and the ATO, 72.8% of individuals that own an investment property own just one. Meanwhile, 18% of individuals owned two, while less than 1% of individuals owned six or more. The breakdown is shown below:

Number of properties	%
1	72.8
2	18
3	5.5
4	2
5	0.8
6 or more	0.9

Table 8: Individuals' interest in rental properties

I can only speculate about why this is. I suspect the majority of people who buy an investment property do it just so that they can tell their family and friends that they have an investment. Then they forget about their investment property and become complacent.

Fortunately, that's how easy it is to own an investment property. Buy it and forget it: the estate agent and property manager will manage it for you. An investment property can simply sit there and without any effort or input from the owner, it will grow in value. Some time down the track, perhaps when the owner is thinking about retiring, they will consider their investment property and wonder how much money they have made and how clever they were to have bought it all those years ago. Only after they have sold the property and seen their bank balance increase will they wonder, "Why didn't I buy another investment property?" and "How much more money would I have if I had bought more of these investments?"

I recommend that you wait 12–18 months before you buy another investment property. For some investors, this may be far too conservative; they might have purchased several investment properties in this time frame. For those readers who are a bit more cautious, the reason I suggest waiting 12–18 months is that, in most cases, it is sufficient time for the real-estate market to have grown in value. After 12 months, you can get a new valuation for your investment property and show your bank how much your equity (wealth) has grown. This equity will help you buy another investment property.

Also, I have personally found that when you have owned an investment property for a period of time, the added activity in your bank account (rent money coming in and loan repayments going out) no longer seems peculiar. Once you get used to the extra activity, you will stop looking at your bank balance and stop worrying about the loan being serviced. You come to realise that the property is taking care of itself. When that happens, you are ready to buy your next investment property.

Step 3. Repeat steps 1 and 2

If you follow this blueprint, in about 10 years you will most likely own around six or seven investment properties. If we assume the average value of each property is between $300,000 and $500,000, your investment portfolio will be worth between $1,800,000 and $3,500,000. In about 10 years, this value will double. What you do next is up to you. But isn't it nice to have options?

Having choices about what you would like to do is one of the most valuable things in life. For this reason, the last message I would like to leave with you is—stop procrastinating and **JUST DO IT!**

Summary

1. *Buy an investment property.* Buy an investment property in the next three months. This is a reasonable time frame. Do your research and make sure you are not paying too much. When you find a suitable property—buy it. Protect yourself with a "subject to bank finance" clause in the contract. The bank will independently value the property when assessing your application for a loan, and if you have overcommitted, that application will be rejected, getting you safely out of the deal.

2. *After 12–18 months, buy another investment property.* This period of 12–18 months is enough for the real-estate market, and your investment, to have risen in value. You may be able to use the increased equity in your investment to secure new finance. By this time, you will also have become used to the added activity in your bank account— from income and expenses associated with the

property—and will feel more confident making your next purchase.

3. *Repeat steps 1 and 2.* It's that simple.

Afterword

Long before I wrote my first book, *How to Buy Unlimited Investment Properties*, I had read several books and attended numerous seminars on property investing. Afterward, I quite naively thought it would be easy to build my own multimillion-dollar investment portfolio. Unfortunately, those books and seminars I attended left gaps in my education and I was not fully prepared for some of the challenges I faced, or the difficulties and disappointments I encountered as a result.

I felt motivated to write a frank account of what I had experienced, including both the successes and the failures, in the hope that readers would be better prepared than I was and could avoid some of the mistakes I made.

I also wanted to inspire readers to buy their own investment properties and most importantly know how to start. From the responses I've received, I'm now pleased to know that I succeeded.

I decided to write this new book after receiving overwhelming support and encouragement from my editor and the people who read *How to Buy Unlim-*

ited Investment Properties. I am extremely grateful to these people for all their kind words and feedback, and I hope that you enjoy this book. Thank you.

The other and more compelling reason for writing *Buy Unlimited Properties and Retire in 10 Years* was that after working as an estate agent for two decades and having my own real estate agency, I continue to be surprised how many property investors have only one investment property, and how many "experienced" investors (who have had their investment property at least a few years) constantly seek advice and second-guess themselves.

It became abundantly clear to me that many people have no clear idea of what to do after they have bought their most important investment. There are a few factors involved, including lack of information and education on the topic of owning multiple properties and how to create money from your portfolio.

Drive is one thing I do *not* believe investors lack. If they didn't want to expand their portfolio or make more money from it, why would they seek advice from their real-estate agent? The key thing missing, as far as I could see, was a practical understanding of what investors should do next, once they have bought that first investment property. This is what I set out to provide.

I took the idea that you could *Retire in 10 Years* as the focus of this book because self-funded retirement is a hot topic today, and the generosity of government-funded pensions is regularly being questioned. It is now vitally important that you look after yourself financially, in the present and in your later years. No one else is responsible for you, and no one else can be relied upon to look after you. You need to take care of yourself.

People understand this, and more and more, they are turning toward real estate as an investment vehicle that they hope will provide for them in their retirement years. In Australia, self-managed super funds have become increasingly popular, in part because they allow direct investment in real estate. Those funds can now also borrow money, which has made a massive difference for many investors, enabling them to build real-estate portfolios with their superannuation.

Buying one investment property is obviously a great start; it can give you a warm, fuzzy feeling inside, and you may feel like you have made it. It might also give you bragging rights among family and friends, as you can proudly announce that you have an investment property. But one day, when you sell your one and only investment property and take your profit, I am sure you will wonder, "why didn't I buy more of these?"

As the past few hundred pages will have made clear, I believe it is absolutely essential that you buy more than one investment property. Unless you are very lucky or prepared to settle for less in your retirement years, one investment property won't provide you with enough passive income to live on. That's the bad news.

The good news, as I have demonstrated here, is that you don't need to own a huge number of properties to be able to retire from work and live happily on a passive income. The amount you can earn passively, in this way, is limited only by your own expectations and the number of investment properties you buy.

Occasionally, you will come across a human interest story in the newspaper or on the television about a stay-at-home mum or other battler who, in a few short years, went from nowhere to owning scores of investment properties, worth millions. These stories can inspire us, but they can also seem daunting, because they sometimes imply that you need lots and lots of investment properties to create substantial wealth.

If you want to buy lots of investment properties, that's fantastic! I have no doubt that if you find the right properties, you can buy an unlimited number. However, you should also consider that the more investment properties you own, the greater the potential for headaches. There are more insurance policies to be paid, you will receive more maintenance requests, and you will need to deal with more property managers and tenants.

I certainly would not try to dissuade you from buying lots and lots of investment properties. My intention is to help you keep in perspective the number of investment properties you need to earn the passive income you desire. If you can keep your goals manageable and achievable, you will be able to take the unwavering, immediate, and decisive action that comes from believing you can achieve what you set out to do. This confidence and decisiveness is absolutely essential for you to reach success. Building a real-estate portfolio is achievable, and not as hard or as daunting as many people think.

The other important thing I would like to help you keep in perspective is the horror stories about terrible tenants that have smashed up rental properties. Everybody knows one of these stories, or has seen them on the TV, but they are not common, and they certainly are not typical of tenants in general. Remember that about one third of all properties are currently being rented. Look around your own neighbourhood on a daily basis, and you see will rental properties all around you. You might not even know which of them are rented and which are owner-occupied. It is not likely that any of the properties in your street have been trashed, and if they are—the people responsible could even be owner-occupiers!

On the basis of your experience, ask yourself—is all the hype and bad press about terrible tenants fair, or are people using these stories as excuses to justify not having bought any investment properties? Some people who have neglected the opportunity to invest perpetuate the stories about terrible tenants because they want to scare others away from buying investment properties. This makes them feel better about themselves and their own shortcomings, and validates their inaction.

From my personal experience, the vast majority of tenants are wonderful people and take good care of the rental property they live in. For the reasons I explained earlier in this book, the best way to ensure your investment property is being well looked after is to use the services of a fully qualified, experienced property manager.

As I've mentioned, you could own lots and lots of investment properties, but you don't have to. If not, how many properties *would* you need to stop working and live comfortably? As we approach the end of this book, please take a moment to consider this question.

You might not be thinking of retiring just yet, but if you could replace your salary with an equivalent passive income that you didn't have to work for, would you quit your job? If I offered to replace your salary with a passive income at the same level as your salary, with the stipulation that you must quit your job, would you take me up on it? How much *would* you need to earn from a passive income before you quit? Would you accept $50,000 a year? $100,000, $150,000, $200,000 … or would you hold out for more?

Before you answer, my advice, again, is to keep it in perspective. If you'd hold out for $200,000 a year, but you currently earn $80,000, are happy with it, and can live comfortably, why do you need to aim for $200,000?

I am not suggesting that you should not aim high. You will have your reasons for wanting an income of $200,000 a year, but be careful—if you set your expectation too high, you may stumble at the first hurdle. Also remember that if you cannot stop working until you have a passive income of $200,000 per year, you may need to keep working longer than you would like.

When you've decided how much money you would have to be offered to quit work, divide it by

$25,000.[7] The answer (the figure you are left with) is the number of debt-free, unencumbered investment properties you need to stop working and retire.

So, if you would like to stop working and have a passive income of $100,000 a year, you need four properties. If you want $150,000, you will need six properties, and so on. Of course, you always have other options, such as re-financing, which I described earlier in this book.

The crucial point is that one investment property is a wonderful start, but it really is only the start. In this book, I have shown you why you should go on and buy as many properties as you need to achieve your goals, and given you the simple, easy-to-follow steps that you need to take action. My hope is that you get out there and do it, so you can achieve financial freedom and make your life what you most want it to be.

---

[7]That number, $25,000, is roughly what you would receive in a year from a property with a weekly rental of $500–$550, less expenses.

Contact the author

Thank you for reading my book. I hope you found it interesting, enjoyable, and helpful. I also hope that it is an affirmation of the things you are doing right and a catalyst for change in areas where you would like to do better.

I would love to hear from any readers who want to discuss the topics covered in my books, or who have any real-estate stories they would like to share. My contact details are provided below.

I promise I will reply to all readers who send me a message; just note that messages must be in English.

I can be contacted at: markreister01@gmail.com and facebook.com/mark.reister.3.

Good luck and happy investing.

—Mark Reister

Also by Mark Reister

How to Buy Unlimited Investment Properties

Before embarking on his property investment journey, real-estate agent Mark Reister attended numerous investment seminars, sitting with everyone from battlers to academics in search of the path that lets some people afford whatever they want.

In the end, Mark decided to forge his own path, developing a strategy that enabled him to secure 13 investment properties in his first 12 months of concerted effort.

How to Buy Unlimited Investment Properties is a step-by-step account of exactly how he built his multi-million-dollar property portfolio—and how you could do the same.

Coming soon

How the Experts Buy Unlimited Properties

In this collection edited by Mark Reister, leading Australian property investors share their knowledge and top tips for creating wealth through property.

www.ingramcontent.com/pod-product-compliance
Lightning Source LLC
Chambersburg PA
CBHW021421170526
45164CB00001B/49